# FAITH

## The FAITH That Pleases God!

# Contents

# Chapter 1
# Dedication

I want to dedicate this book to the Lord God Almighty, my best-best-best friend. There are not enough words and not enough time.

To Noelle, my best-best friend, without whom I cannot breathe on the earth.

And I want to dedicate this book to all the rest of my best friends.

My radio friends (actually family)... All the people that have had the privilege to get to know all over the world and beyond you make the ministry worth doing when you make laying at treasures for heaven a lot easier

Don Crawford Jr. - an outstanding and fascinating friend who has helped me prevail in ministry at levels I didn't even imagine.

Rob and Cindy Lafler: my life's great prayer warriors.

The KPW (which stands for Kingdom Prayer Warriors): you know each of you and who you are.

To every person who will read or hear this book and take one step closer to the Lord in faith, may the Lord bless you on your journey a thousandfold.

# Chapter 2
# Introduction

This is the third book that I've written, and I sincerely hope it brings you joy and fulfillment. This book is designed to inspire and strengthen your faith.

Throughout my life, there have been moments when I felt overwhelmed by circumstances. However, I always find comfort in the grace and mercy bestowed upon me by God's love.

I have come to realize that faith grants me access to God, thanks to the redemptive work of Jesus Christ on the cross. Faith is what God desires from us. **Faith in God has the power to transform anything and everything.**

I hope that you, like me, seek to discover the profound significance of stepping out in faith, just as Peter did when he walked on water towards Jesus. This decision to put our faith in the Lord is always the right one.

It is my sincere desire to deepen my love for God and please Him, for without faith, it is impossible to do so. May we all walk with unwavering faith in our Lord, with our hearts and minds.

# Chapter 3
# Faith...From My Perspective

I want to say something about faith. The first thing I want to say is it's often radical. You have acknowledged that Jesus Christ is the Son of the living God who died on the cross, was buried, and rose again three days later. You know that happened 2,000 years ago, right? Yet you believe. You might not consider that radical, but somebody who does not operate in faith would consider that radical.

You believe. You've prayed prayers to an unseen God and then manifested the answers so you can see them. Isn't that powerful? I want you to really catch this. You are radical in your faith, and you should be. You should recognize that. You believe in Jesus Christ, who lived 2,000 years ago, died on the cross, and rose again three days later. You believe that. You weren't there, yet your faith says, "Yes."

Faith is often radical, and every one of you has radical faith. I know you don't think of it as radical. "I didn't put my foot out over the boat." Yes, you did because you're saying Jesus is alive 2,000 years later. That's the foot over the boat. Okay?

Faith is not just radical. I want you to really understand this. Faith has an expectancy. Many people think that you pray, and then you've done your job by praying. Then you don't even think about it again or address it or whatever the case may be. Let me say something that I think is important, coming out of Mark 11:20-24.

*"In the morning, as they went along, they saw the fig tree withered from the roots. Peter remembered and said to Jesus, 'Rabbi, look! The fig tree you cursed has withered!' 'Have faith in God,' Jesus answered. 'Truly I tell you, if anyone says to this mountain, "Go, throw yourself into the sea," and does not doubt in their heart but believes that what they say will happen, it will be done for them. Therefore I tell you, whatever you ask for in prayer, believe that you have received it, and it will be yours.'"*

Now, is that "name it and claim it"? No. Stop that. But when you pray, there should be an expectancy that God answers, unlike the early church. In Acts 12, The Disciples prayed for Peter to be delivered. When Peter knocked on the door, they all said, "No, it isn't him," even though they had prayed and asked God to deliver Peter. God said, "Okay. Here's the answer," Peter came knocking on the door, and they said, "Nope. It's not him. Nope. Don't believe it," because they had lost any sense of expectancy.

Just because we are two thousand plus years past these people doesn't mean we don't do the exact same thing. When you pray, there has to be an expectancy. The Lord is responding to your prayer. He's not looking for you to pray and then walk away and go, "Eh, whatever. I threw up a prayer. Who knows. It could happen. Maybe will, maybe won't."

I'll share something with you. I've mentioned this before. I remember being a young Christian, and my faith was on fire. I was told that I needed to get a job. I won't tell you who told me, and I won't tell you how I was told. Let's just say somebody in my family said, "Get a job or get out." So I said, "Man, I've got to get a job."

So, what would you do when you were looking for a job in 1978? You would grab the classifieds, and you would look at them and read them and say, "Okay. I'm going to find a job." This actually happened. I said, "You know, I'm going to pray for a job, and I'm going to ask God to bring me a job." Isn't that crazy? Yes, it's crazy. So I closed the newspaper, and I prayed.

I said, "Lord, I ask you to bring me a job. I don't know how. I don't know how it should be. I don't know if it's from the past or whatever. Just please bring me a job." I dressed and walked out the front door of my house in Phoenix, Arizona. Ben, who had a landscaping company and was cutting the grass right by the front door, as I walked out said, "Hey, Dave, do you need a job?" I said, "Yes." He goes, "Okay. You can start tomorrow."

I know you're thinking, "No!" Wrong. That's exactly what happened. I worked for Ben, by the way, on and off for the next two and a half years. A great guy, a Christian man. I didn't know it at the time. Let me explain something to you. Prayer does work, and faith is real. Even if we (let me say this big theological term) pooh-pooh it from time to time, God loves genuine faith and responds to it.

So, we talked about faith being radical, and you're radical. We talked about faith having an expectancy. Some of you go, "I have faith, Dave. I have faith." God knows whether the faith is genuine or not. He knows whether you're really having it or just saying it. It's not up to me. It's not my call. You know whether you have faith. God knows better than you whether you have faith.

Here's one thing I want to tell you about faith, though. Listen to this statement. **<u>Faith operates outside of perfection</u>**. There is something in the mind of the Christian that he/she has to fight to receive grace. Grace is something God gives us. *Grace* actually means unmerited favor. You can't earn it. It can't be deserved. You'll hear people on television and in movies go, "Well, I deserve some grace." No, you can never deserve grace. Grace is unmerited. It doesn't matter what the world says.

So, many Christians struggle just to receive their salvation. Grace is given in the process of salvation. It's received by faith, and then it's realized after you receive it by faith, but it's given by grace, unmerited favor. Faith operates for Christians when they're praying. Again, the same principle is at play whether you're praying on a regular basis or when you're praying about something really important.

In Galatians 3:5, Paul wrote, ***"So again I ask, does God give you his Spirit and work miracles among you by the works of the law, or by your believing what you heard?"*** It's as plain as can be, even if you're using a Good News Translation or something else. Does God work miracles among you, does He answer your prayers, does He give you His Spirit because you are obedient or because you have faith? The answer is God does wondrous things because you have faith.

You think, "Well, a person of faith should have all these different characteristics." It opens the door for things you cannot anticipate or accomplish. Faith opens that door in ways you cannot even anticipate.

As John Piper said, as C.S. Lewis said, and as many other great people have said, God has more tunnels, more methods, more ways, more transports, more delivery systems than any human being could ever, ever imagine, and faith accesses that. So, you pray for something and think, "Oh, well, whatever," or you pray for it and expect it, and you know it's a little radical. But we don't sit there and examine ourselves **to allow the doubt to eliminate the faith**.

I'm talking about practical Christian living. You pray a prayer, lift it up before the Lord, walk away, and then say, "I'm not worthy of that one being answered." Wrong. Wrong. Wrong. Wrong answer because that's not what it's based on. It's based on your faith. It's based on your ability to believe. It's based on your ability to believe that God is generous and that He's a Giver, not because you're a perfect person.

You know what? I don't want to break it to you in too many ways, but practically, you're not a perfect person. Except for the righteousness of Jesus Christ (positionally), you'd be gone. That faith opens doors and creates opportunities for the divine to show provision. That's what you want to be operating in. That's what pleases God.

Keep in mind this perspective on faith... Faith is radical (1), faith is expectant (2), and faith operates outside of perfection (3). And faith opens doors (4). There are ways God responds to our faith that we have not even imagined how has put things together, but He requires faith to please him. Now, some people will ask, "Well, why?" Here's the best theological answer: because that's the method God has chosen.

God has chosen faith as the vehicle by which to engage with him. "Well, He doesn't have to." Right. He doesn't, but He did, and that's what we have. You can either operate by faith under God's system or not. That's the wonderful thing. People say, "Well, it should be like *this*" or "It should be like *that*." Well, when you become God, you switch the system. Until then, be quiet and do what He wants.

Again, faith is radical, expectant, operates outside of perfection, and opens doors. Here's another thing. I will use Jesus' words because He says ***them better than I do: "Then Jesus told his disciples a parable to show them that they should always pray and not give up. He said, 'In a certain town, there was a judge who neither feared God nor cared what people thought.'"*** He's telling a story about a guy who couldn't care less about God.

*"'And there was a widow in that town who kept coming to him with the plea, "Grant me justice against my adversary." For some time refused. But finally said to himself, "Even though I don't fear God or care what people think, yet because this widow keeps bothering me, I will see that she gets justice so that she won't eventually come and attack me!"'*

*And the Lord said, 'Listen to what the unjust judge says. And will not God bring about justice for his chosen ones, who cry out to him day and night? Will keep putting them off? I tell you, will see that they get justice, and quickly. However, when the Son of Man comes, will find faith on the earth?'"*

Now, the primary explanation of *"When the Son of Man comes, will find faith?"* has to do with the return of Jesus Christ, but don't misunderstand the context. He's giving a parable on how people should pray and not give up, and they should keep on praying. They're asking for specifics and petitions.

Jesus says, **"When the Son of Man comes, will  find faith?"** When you pray, your prayer goes out of your mouth and goes up to heaven... When God comes to respond to your prayer, will you still have faith when He does, or did you drop that? Do you get that? Let that sink in for a second. In context, he's talking about how people should pray and not give up.

Then says, "When the Son of Man comes, will He find faith on the earth?" Now, again, the primary, without any question, without any doubt whatsoever, has to do with the return of Jesus Christ, but I will just ask this question in general. When you pray a prayer and the Lord goes to respond, do you still have the faith you offered the prayer up with, or has that fallen?

**This is why prayer is more than a moment; it's a way of life.** This is why faith is more than a moment; it's a way of life. This is why hope is more than a moment; it's a way of life. This is why love is more than a moment; it's a way of life. This is why the Christian existence is more than a moment; it's a way of life. Second Corinthians 5:7 says, ***"For we live by faith, not by sight."*** We're supposed to live this way.

In normal life, if you're driving down the road and close your eyes when driving, what will happen? You're going to crash, because you have to see to go down the road. Well, in Christianity, that driving process requires faith to see. In other words, it's like you're driving in your car of faith; you put your glasses on, and you have to see that way to see the road. If you drove down the freeway and closed your eyes... Especially when they merge. You're going to become part of the barrier. Come on, man.

You need to have faith to see to drive down the roadway that God has intended for you. You have to look at it with faith. If you're a person who has poor eyesight, kind of like I do reading... If I don't put my glasses on, I can't read. You need your Jesus glasses to believe. Put those right ones on so you can see the right thing, so it's clear, and not everything looks so jumbled.

That's actually what happens to me. Everything looks smooshed together when I try to read something without my glasses. When I put my glasses on, I can make that distinction. Put your Jesus faith glasses on in your situation, in your circumstance. You live by faith. You don't just momentarily shoot faith up in the air and go, "Whatever." You live by it.

You're sitting there thinking, "Dave, that's like pie in the sky." Okay. I'll tell Jesus that's pie in the sky because that's what Jesus said to do. You think, "Well, where did say that?" We just did Luke 18:1-8. We just did Mark 11:20-24. I didn't even quote Matthew 14:22-31 or Matthew 14:15-21. We didn't even touch Ephesians 3:20. It's filled with it.

It's impossible to please God without faith. We've got to walk that way. You say, "Okay. I'll try to have more faith." No, I want you to **live** with more faith, not just have a moment of more faith. Live with it. Wake up with it and go to bed with it. That would be pleasing to God. All of the things we try to do... Not many on the list would make Him happy, but faith is one of them. He loves that. Okay? Let's pray.

# Chapter 4
# The Faith Place

The title of this chapter is *The Faith Place*. I want to read the biblical definition of faith in Hebrews 11:1. ***"Now faith is being sure of what we hope for and certain of what we do not see."***

There are two definitions given in Hebrews 11:1 for faith. Many people take this and say this is one long definition. No, it's not. It's two separate definitions. It's two separate things.

The conjunction **"and"** combines the first process, definition, and thought with the second process and thought. These are two definitions of what faith is.

Faith is being sure of what we hope for, being solid about what we're hoping for, and being so confident of what we're hoping for. When you function in that principle, in that aspect, that is faith, according to the Bible.

The second definition is to be certain of what we do not see. We are absolutely certain of what we do not see. We do not see heaven, yet we are certain it will be there because of our faith. That's what faith is.

The best example in the universe that I could ever think of whenever you're talking about faith is David and Goliath, which is a classic demonstration of faith. It's David hearing Goliath being defiant to the armies of Israel. Goliath stood at least 9'2". We've talked about this before. I don't know how many people think Shaquille O'Neal is a big guy. He's about 7'2" and 300 pounds. I mean, he's a massive human being, even among athletes.

Now imagine a guy who's a warrior. He's not a seamstress; he's a warrior, and he's over nine feet tall! This is a huge being. This is an enormous entity. David looks at Goliath and says, "No. You're dishonoring the name of my God. I don't like this situation. This is changing right now. I'm going to have to take you out."

You just have to perceive this six-foot guy, and this nine-foot guy and the six-foot guy can only see, "You've got to go, pal. You are checking out. You're defying God. It's not working for me." That is faith.

He could only see himself conquering Goliath. He could see it no other way. He couldn't process it any other way. We all understand faith from time to time. You hear an inspiring message on faith, and we often talk about it. Most of what we deal with are Goliath-style situations where we feel like we're David and Goliath is the situation, and we need to have faith in order to get through our Goliath.

Faith, by and large, as we discuss it amongst ourselves and in church, is situational. It's based on the situations we encounter. **But not today. This day, faith is going to be relational, not situational**.

You think, "What?" We will review the requirements of faith relationship-wise, not situation-wise, because we're supposed to have faith in our relationships. Look at Hebrews 11:6. Let's look at the first person we're supposed to have a relational faith interaction with.

***"And without faith, it is impossible to please God..."*** If we could have that tattooed on our foreheads, we'd all be doing much better. "You know, I'd really like to make God happy." Really? Well, then start believing. "Oh. Really? Is that what...?" Yeah. See? That's what it says. ***"...because anyone who comes to Him must believe that He exists and rewards those who earnestly seek him."***

So, the first person we are supposed to have faith in regarding a relationship is God. As the scriptures command, we're supposed to believe that as we come to God in faith, that pleases Him. We petition with our petition. When you do that, you must believe He exists, or why would you ask him? Then, if you believe He exists, you're also required by Scripture to believe He rewards those who earnestly seek Him and that God responds to that.

The biggest issue, or the biggest problem, is that people don't understand **God is a <u>GIVER</u>**!

So, what we're talking about is faith, and we're not talking about faith situationally; we're talking about faith relationally, and the first person we're talking about regarding that relationship is God. We need to have faith in God. Not just that it will all work out for good; we need to have faith in who He is. Again, who is He? **He is a <u>GIVER</u>**!

Matthew 7:7: "Ask..." There's a start. That's the big problem in this relationship with God. God starts the whole thing, saying, "Hey, you should ask Me. You should ask Me." We're like, "Well, we'll do everything we can, and we'll get everything done that we can, and when we've run out of every possible resource, then we'll go to prayer." God is going, "Hello! Look up here. Look up here. Look up here." I mean, we just don't do it. We don't ask first. We do ask last. Why? Everybody knows why. <u>We're dumb</u>. That's why.

*"Ask, and it will be given to you; seek, and you will find; knock, and the door will be opened to you. For everyone who asks receives; he who seeks finds; and to him who knocks, the door will be opened. Which of you, if his son asks for bread, will give him a stone? Or if he asks for a fish, will give him a snake? If you, then, though you are evil, know how to give good gifts to your children, how much more will your Father in heaven give good gifts to those who ask him!"*

One of the first things we need to somehow imprint somewhere in all our gray matter is **God is a GIVER**, that He gives to His children, that He loves to give to His children. Jesus uses the illustration that if your child came up to you and said, "I want a piece of bread; I'm hungry," it's not like you're going to go, "Oh, here, have a rattlesnake." No, you're not like that, and you're evil.

So, if that's the case, then let's just put God in the picture. How much more is God going to give to His kids who have needs? How much better at parenting is God than us? A "gabazillion." (That's a new number. I just made it up. It's a big one, whatever it is.) The idea is to understand that we need to have faith in **God as a GIVER** in our relationship with Him.

This is not the "I'm going to pull teeth with God to get an answered prayer" process of Christianity. "Well, if I do just enough juggling and just enough dancing, I think God will respond." That is not what's supposed to happen. We are supposed to believe **He is a GIVER**, use that faith, come to Him, and trust that He rewards those who diligently pursue Him. That's the first one: faith in God. The second is a little tougher.

The first person we're supposed to have faith in is God. That's the first faith place, but the second person we're supposed to have faith in or faith for, so to speak, is ***other believers***. Faith in others and faith for others. You think, "Are you sure we're supposed to have faith in other believers?" As sure as I am... that Genesis 1:1 through Revelation 22:21 is the Word of God. Yes, I am sure.

First Corinthians 13:7. We'll go to verse 4 as the lead-up so you understand what it's saying. ***"Love is patient, love is kind. It does not envy, it does not boast, it is not proud. It is not rude; it is not self-seeking; it is not easily angered, and it keeps no record of wrongs. Love does not delight in evil but rejoices with the***

***truth. It always protects, always trusts, always hopes, always perseveres.*** *"* Love believes. There is faith that operates in the principle of love.

So, we're told to love God with all our heart, all our soul, all our strength, and all our mind. That's our first commandment. Our second commandment is to love our neighbor as we love ourselves. We're supposed to love others, and in that love is a faith, a belief. Let me redefine that. What that means, which we rarely do, or at least very rarely acknowledge...

It means we're supposed to interpret what people say and do with faith, not cynicism. I'm a little more cynical than most, and I acknowledge that sinfulness. It could be part of my upbringing and part of my painful church past. I'm sure nobody else has ever been hurt in a church, so you wouldn't understand.

The idea is to understand that what is required of us in Scripture is to believe the best about someone's actions. Do you know what we do? We believe the worst and make them prove the best because we don't believe them. Here's the kicker. Here's the thing you'll hate the most. The main point is we're supposed to trust Christ in each other. Ooh, you're supposed to do what? You're supposed to trust the Christ in one another (Love one another).

When you're around brothers and sisters, is Jesus in you only, or is He in you and them too? Do we have no confidence in the Christ who lives in them? Ow! Take the dagger out of my back anytime you want. That's very painful. Now I'll tell my story, which some have heard several times and you will hear again.

Fret not. It's about interpreting incorrectly. It is something I do very well. I do it probably better than all of you. Seriously.

I'm in church, and I'm preaching on the basic tenets of the faith. If you know me at all, I am a conservative charismatic. I believe every word in that book. I am a die-hard Bible thumper who believes that all the book is applicable, but I do believe there's a new covenant and an old covenant, so I'm not stuck in the ceremonial laws or something for the Old Testament.

I'm up there preaching in church, and I'm preaching about the death, burial, resurrection, and absolute certainty of the return of Jesus Christ. It's hard to get more basic than those Bible truths. Bam! Bam! Bam! I'm preaching away and preaching away. In the audience is a woman, and every time I'm making a major point... And, boy, I'm ferocious. You know, spit is flying. It's one of those sermons that are dangerous for people in the front rows...She's in her seat, shaking her head back and forth. I'm like, "Grrrrrrr!"

Instead of feeling I should approach this differently, I get more ferocious. So now I'm really preaching. I'm really going after it. "Jesus is Lord! He's coming back, and what you think doesn't matter!" She just keeps shaking her head back and forth. I'm thinking, "I can't wait until church is over and I can meet this woman. Yeah. I'm going to have it out with her right here in church."

I keep preaching, and she keeps shaking her head. Service is over, and I make a beeline for this woman because I can't wait to see what she has to say. It's Victor's aunt, and Victor stands up and says, "Hi, Pastor Dave. I'd like you to meet my aunt. She doesn't speak English."

What?

She doesn't speak English.

That ruined *that* whole thing.

I am such an idiot.

Why? Because my confidence level or trust in Christ for her was zero, and my interpretive skills were apparently zero that day. And, oh yeah, that thing where you're supposed to be led by the Lord? I must have just forgotten it because it wasn't active at all. It shows you how we can quickly interpret, misinterpret, or misconstrue what people think, say, or do because we don't believe the best in people.

I've said this before, and if I offended you, I apologize now. You must forgive me because if you don't, you're in trouble with God.

The truth of the matter is you walk in the door, and you meet somebody you've seen a hundred times. You've shaken their hand a hundred times, and the hundred and first time you go to shake their hand, they turn away or go a different direction, and immediately the Devil comes in and says, "Well, this person is snobby. This person is this and *this*." It could just be that that person feels off (too many tacos the night before?) and is going in the other direction. You don't know, but in your mind, you're thinking, "Oh, they're too good for me." We go through that thought process.

What is that? That is us having no faith in others. That's what it is. Isn't that tough? I'm not preaching just to you. I'm most definitely preaching to me. That's how it goes. It's true.

So, the first person we're supposed to have faith in is <u>God</u>. The second person we're supposed to have faith in is <u>other believers</u>. Ah, but there's a third person I want to talk to you about that you're supposed to have faith in. There's a little catch on this.

So, in The Faith Place. We're talking about faith—relational faith, faith in God, faith in others. Now we're talking about the third and final person where that faith is supposed to go, which is faith in **yourself**. You think, "Faith in yourself?" Relax. You know I will get there through the Scriptures, so take a deep breath and relax.

Matthew 4:1: ***"Then Jesus was led by the Spirit into the desert to be tempted by the devil. After fasting forty days and forty nights, he was hungry. The tempter came to him and said, 'If you are the Son of God, tell these stones to become bread.'"***

Stop. You don't have to go any farther than that. The Devil is not an idiot. His task is to thwart your faith in God as best as he can. He can't completely do that, but it's his goal, so to speak.

His other goal is to thwart your faith in other believers. He does a little better at that, actually, in church life than most people would acknowledge. His third goal is to thwart your faith in any capacity you might have in your own faith-conquering walk. You think, "What are you talking about?" Verse 3 is a perfect example of what I'm talking about. Look at what the Devil says to Jesus. The audacity of Satan to say this is outstanding.

*"The tempter came to him and said, 'If you are the Son of God, tell these stones to become bread.'"* The Devil shoots self-doubt even to the Son of God. *"If you are the Son of God..."* I kind of wish Jesus would have gone, "Well if I'm not, what are you doing here dropping these temptations on me?" You almost wish there was some kind of response like that. But look at what the Enemy is doing. He's challenging who Jesus is. He doesn't say, "Because you're the Son of God." He says, *"If you're the Son of God..."*

You think, "Well, how does that apply to me?" It's the same temptation you go through when the Devil says to you, "If you are a child of God..." Oh, you're a child of God, but that doesn't mean the Enemy is not going to drop it in there and make you doubt it. "Are you really a child of God? Are you really saved? I don't know. You kind of do a bunch of sins. You know that. I know that. God knows that. Do you really think you're His?"

It's that little subtlety he drops in there as he tries to rearrange your thinking about yourself: "Well, I don't do this perfectly." Then, all of a sudden, you're in an engaged conversation in Insanity-Land, which has nothing to do with truth whatsoever. Perfect is Jesus. Perfect is you in Jesus. That's it. Nothing more.

The Devil drops that exact same thing in our own laps. "If you're a child of God..." "Oh, if you were really a daughter of God, you would..." "If you're really a son of the Most High God, wouldn't you...?" That's what he drops in your direction.

That's the Devil's take on it. He tries to instill that doubt. I just want to refer to this passage I want to read. This is not a "name it and claim it" passage, because we don't believe in that, per se, but we do believe in **scriptural, biblical,** *"It says it; let's use it."* So, let's turn to biblical Mark, chapter 9.

I want God's take on this. I want to drill this from a particular point. I want you to follow what we will do in this Mark chapter 9 passage. It's very interesting because it comes down to answering a critical, key question.

Let's start with verse 21. This is in reference to the boy with the evil spirit they bring to Jesus after He comes down off the Mount of Transfiguration. Verse 21: ***"Jesus asked the boy's father, 'How long has he been like this?' 'From childhood,' he answered. 'It has often thrown him into fire or water to kill him. But if you can do anything, take pity on us and help us.' '"If you can"?' said Jesus. 'Everything is possible for him who believes.'"***

***"Everything is possible for him who believes."*** I didn't write it. With God, everything is possible for us because we're His children. Caveat: with God, everything is possible. So, on a day-by-day basis, as Christians, here is the critical key and question that is asked every day and must be answered every day...every single day. Whom do we agree with...God or the Devil? You must answer that question every day.

If you let him drop an "**if**" in your life, you agree with him, the enemy. If you stand as the child of God that God ordained you to be, you agree with God. Every day, you have to decide who you're going to agree with: the Devil or the Lord. I'm going to give you the answer.

You don't have to turn there, because you know it's true, and you can look it up in a minute.

The answer comes from the apostle Paul in Philippians 4:13, which we should also tattoo on our foreheads. Paul says, ***"I can do all things through him who strengthens me."*** So, the answer to that everyday question... Every day you wake up, you should start the day with Philippians 4:13. **"I can do everything through Jesus. Whatever happens, I can do this through Jesus. Period."**

So, it's not just faith towards God (1). It's not just faith towards others (2). It's also faith towards ourselves (3) in our partnership with God. Some may say, "Well, that sounds like arrogance." Nope. The difference between that and truth is arrogance is a sin, but confidence is a command. Hebrews 10:35 says, ***"Don't throw away your confidence, which will be richly rewarded."***

The difference between confidence and arrogance is... "I can do all things because I'm awesome" is arrogance. **<u>"I can do all things through Jesus because He's awesome," is confidence.</u>**

That's the difference between the two. In closing, here it is. Let's use faith no matter who we deal with, including God, other believers, and ourselves, for we are children of the Most High God. Let's pray.

# Chapter 5
# We Gotta Believe... To See

The title of this chapter is *We Gotta Believe to See*. Christianity is the weirdest faith there can be. To live, you have to die. To receive, you have to give. To see, you have to believe. Normally, in life, it's "I'll believe it when I see it," but Christianity is no; you do not see it until you believe it. That's the call. That's the way God does it. So, let's look at Mark, chapter 10, starting in verse 46. It says the following.

*"Then they came to Jericho. As Jesus and his disciples, together with a large crowd, were leaving the city, a blind man, Bartimaeus (that is, the Son of Timaeus), was sitting by the roadside begging. When he heard that it was Jesus of Nazareth, he began to shout, 'Jesus, Son of David, have mercy on me!' Many rebuked him and told him to be quiet, but he shouted all the more, 'Son of David, have mercy on me!'*

*Jesus stopped and said, 'Call him.' So they called to the blind man, 'Cheer up! On your feet! He's calling you.' Throwing his cloak aside, he jumped to his feet and came to Jesus. 'What do you want me to do for you?' Jesus asked him. The blind man said, 'Rabbi, I want to see.' 'Go,' said Jesus, 'your faith has healed you.' Immediately, he received his sight and followed Jesus along the road."*

Small text. Not a major deal. This is actually the last recorded creative miracle Mark records in his gospel, aside from the resurrection. They were coming from Jericho, which was probably the new Jericho. There was an old Jericho and a new Jericho. The old Jericho dealt with Joshua. The new Jericho was the one that Herod the Great built. They were probably coming from that direction.

They're coming along, and they're walking. They're in their procession, in their group, and all going down the street, and suddenly... Let's look at verse 46. It says, *"As Jesus and his disciples, together with a large crowd, were leaving the city, a blind man, Bartimaeus (that is, the Son of Timaeus), was sitting by the roadside begging. When he heard that it was Jesus of Nazareth, he began to shout, 'Jesus, Son of David, have mercy on me!'"*

The blind man can tell this procession is going around. He finds out it's Christ, and he shouts. He's crying out from within his very being. He's not whispering. He's being loud. He says, "Jesus, Son of David!" Do you know what that means? That means this guy knew Jesus was the Christ. He recognized Christ as the Messiah, Christ as the Savior. He knew this was Jesus.

Now, he might not have known every single thing about Jesus, or all the theology he was supposed to know, but a blind man sitting there, hearing about a man going throughout the regions and healing people... That would have gotten to the blind man. He would have heard that rumor. "Oh, this guy heals people."

"What's his name?"

"Jesus of Nazareth. He's the Messiah. He's the Son of David."

That guy must have been thinking, "Boy, if I ever find *that* guy, I'm going to get ahold of that guy, because I'm blind." He says, "Jesus! Jesus!" He cries out to him. Then he says, "Have mercy." That's *eleeō* in the Greek. What it means is, "Be kind to me." How many of us, when praying to God, say, "Eleeō. Be kind to me. Help!" It is the prayer of help. It's the best prayer in the world. Whenever you're praying before the Lord and don't know what to say, "Help" is great. "Help!"

Sometimes you don't even know what to pray, and the Holy Spirit has to pray for you and intercede for you because you don't know what to pray, but when you're standing there and don't know what to say, and you're before God, just go, "Help." He knows. He knows what it is. He knows what the problem is. He'll respond to that prayer. "*Eleeō.* Help!"

I want you to see what happens in verse 48. It's kind of a shame because this comes from other believers. Oh, that's so sad. Back up to verse 47. ***"When he heard that it was Jesus of Nazareth, he began to shout, 'Jesus, Son of David, have mercy on me!' Many rebuked him and told him to be quiet..."*** The people who rebuked him were not unbelievers. They were the people walking with Jesus.

Do you know what happens a lot? Christians say to other Christians what they think they know is right for them. Have you ever noticed that Christians are always experts for other Christians? Isn't that amazing? They know what another Christian should do. Whether they're doing it or not is irrelevant. They just know. Other Christians will put stuff on you.

This guy was a beggar, and they were saying, "Be quiet. Shut up. You're a beggar. You're not worthy. Be quiet. Don't be spouting out after the Messiah. You're just a beggar on the side of the road." Some Christians will even say to other Christians, "Stop your whining. Stop complaining. Are you blind? Accept your situation. Accept your circumstances. That's the circumstance God put you in. Just accept it. Just deal with it. Stop complaining about it."

Other Christians will put on you, "It's not dignified to shout. It's not dignified to shout out to God like that. That's the Messiah. That's not a very polite way to be a Christian. You should know better than that." But what does Bartimaeus do? It says in verse 48, *"...but he shouted all the more..."* Let me tell you something about being a dignified Christian. It's not very impressive to God to be a dignified Christian.

Do you know what a dignified Christian is? They don't rock the boat, shout, or do something really weird. They just sit there, get dressed, go to church, and nod; when the church is over, they go home and go about their life. That's a dignified Christian. Do you know how impressed God is with that? Zero. Zip-a-dee-dip. None. God is not impressed with dignified people. Do you know what God wants? God wants radicals.

You think, "Dave, you're insane." Really? Let's just talk about King David in 2 Samuel when he's dancing before the Lord. The Bible says with all of his might, he's dancing before the Lord. After dancing with all his might, he gets into the house, and his wife says, "Huh. That was a fairly impressive display you gave. That was very undignified."

David replied, "I was doing that before God with all of my might, and if that's not good enough, I will be more undignified before the Lord. I will do whatever it takes to tell God I love him. I will do whatever it takes to get God's attention. I will do whatever it takes to touch base with my God." God's response was that He shut up David's wife's womb so she couldn't have children.

God liked the fact that David wasn't so dignified. "I'm so dignified I won't do anything." That's not impressive. Anything in the world that stops you from getting God's attention should be eliminated from your life. Anything that detracts you from calling out to God and saying, "*Eleeō*. Be kind to me. Help me..." Anything that stops you from doing that is bad. You need to ignore it.

You need to ignore people who put their Christian spin on you. "This is how you should be a Christian. Like *this*." Hey, I've got a message for you. I'm a pastor, teaching people how to be a Christian. Ready? Don't listen to anybody; follow God. Don't listen to any person; go after God with every ounce you've got. Make it your passion and your life until everybody else... That's what you do because that's what God wants from you.

He wants you to pursue him. He loves to be pursued. God loves to be asked for. God loves to be hunted down, so to speak. Have you ever noticed it says, ***"Ask and you will receive"***? But God wants you to keep on asking. Why does God want you to keep on asking? When Jesus told his disciples to pray, why did He say, "Pray and never give up"? Because He wants you to keep going after God. Don't stop. Don't be complacent in your Christianity. You have never arrived.

"Oh, I've arrived. I go to church. I read my Bible. I do everything I'm supposed to do." Really? You're just like Jesus? Wow! You and Jesus, because there isn't anybody else who's doing that. You're perfect in everything, doing exactly what the Father wants every moment of every day. You've arrived there? I want to hang out with you, then. You see? You're never going to arrive. You keep going. You keep striving. You keep growing.

Pursue after God, passionately, undignified. Who cares? When you die, if you go, "Well, I was well dressed," do you think God is going to go, "Oh, that's great. Come on in"? I don't think so. I think God will go, "I wanted you to want me." God doesn't want you to do anything for anybody; He wants you to do it for Him. He wants you to love Him.

So, this blind man, a better example than I could ever be to you, says, "I'll shout all the more. I will not cease pursuing God." Don't you love that? I wish I had that tenacity. You know, people are telling me, "You shouldn't do *this*. Dave, you shouldn't wear shorts to church, especially on Christmas." Too late. What do you want? It's like, "Well, that's not very dignified." I don't care.

I'm telling you, I'm working on the inside. I'll start working on the outside as soon as I get the inside all squared away. Don't worry. But I've got a long way to go, so relax. It's going to be a while. You know, I want to talk about that. I don't want to belabor this point, but it is important. I want you to turn with me really quickly to Mark, chapter 5. I just want you to see something about this ignoring them thing. I know it sounds kind of rude, but it's not. It's biblical. I want you to look at verse 21 in Mark, chapter 5.

*"When Jesus had again crossed over by boat to the other side of the lake, a large crowd gathered around him while he was by the lake. Then one of the synagogue rulers, named Jairus, came there. Seeing Jesus, he fell at his feet and pleaded earnestly with him, 'My little daughter is dying. Please come and put your hands on her so that she will be healed and live.' So Jesus went with him."*

It's not a tough story, but I want you to go to verse 35. This is the real key right here: *"While Jesus was still speaking, some men came from the house of Jairus, the synagogue ruler. 'Your daughter is dead,' they said. 'Why bother the teacher anymore?'"* Look at verse 36. *"Ignoring what they said, Jesus told the synagogue ruler, 'Don't be afraid; just believe.'"* Jesus is even ignoring what people say.

"Hey, I'm going to follow God."

"Yes, but conventional wisdom..."

"I don't care about conventional wisdom."

"Yes, but you're supposed to be dignified."

"I don't care about being dignified."

"Well, you're supposed to accept your circumstance."

"I don't care about my circumstances."

"Well, you're not worthy."

"I don't care if I'm not worthy. I am going to pursue God. That's what I'm going to do."

I love that. I love the tenacity in that attitude. All right. Back to Mark 10:49 and Bartimus. ***"Many rebuked him and told him to be quiet, but he shouted all the more, 'Son of David, have mercy on me!' Jesus stopped and said, 'Call him.' So they called to the blind man, 'Cheer up! On your feet! He's calling you.'"***

So, the same guys who were saying, "Shut up," are now saying, "Cheer up." It's one of those classics... "Jesus doesn't want to talk to you. Jesus doesn't want to talk to you. Oh, wait...Jesus wants to talk to you." It's like, "Oh, wrong again, are you? Wow, that's amazing." It's just funny how that works.

***"Throwing his cloak aside, he jumped to his feet and came to Jesus."*** Here's where we come to the heart of the message. ***"Throwing his cloak aside..."*** It's not *that* boring. A cloak is a garment for the blind that says they need extra help and care. So, he has this cloak, and he's sitting there. Jesus walks by, he cries out, and Jesus says, "Come here." The Bible says he throws off the cloak. I want you to listen to this. Literally, he throws it off. Anything that slows us down from approaching Jesus should be tossed.

Now, this man had a medical cloak on for blindness, and the medical cloak was saying, "I'm a blind man; take care of me" or "Help me." What the guy did was he tossed it off of him. Many of us have something in our lives that we hold on to, like a cloak of blindness, that says, "I'm inferior. I'm wounded. I'm *this*. I'm *that*. I'm *this*. Take extra care of me." Do you know what this guy did? He took this cloak and threw it off of him. He got rid of it, and he stood up to stand before Christ.

Do you know what a lot of us need to do? We have things in our lives that are like that cloak, and we need to take that little cloak that says, "I need extra help," and we need to go, "Later. I'm following Christ." The bottom line to the message and the key is. Basically, he throws off the old. You've got to love this. He throws off what he was. He throws it off, approaches Christ, and prepares to receive the new. He literally prepares to receive the new.

Here's the crux of the message. Philippians 3:13. The apostle Paul said, ***"This one thing I do: forgetting what is behind me and pressing forward to what is before me."*** There comes a point in your Christian walk where what was in the past needs to be in the past and let go of because today is a new day.

I want to challenge you to walk out onto Main Street after this service ends, and I want you to walk down the middle of the road. And I want you to walk forward, looking backward, and tell me how it goes when the cars hit you while you're looking backward. I want you to do that because when you hold on to the past when the past is still your present, you are walking forward, looking backward, with no idea of what will happen here. None. That is <u>NOT</u> (yes, that is shouting) how God wants you to walk.

If you're a person who speaks every time... Something happens, and you go, "If only *this* would have happened. If only *that*. If only I had done this. If only they would have done *that*." You are a person who is mired in bitterness and disappointment. You should never be saying, "If only." You should say, "Next time I will do *this*, and next time it will be *that*, and next time I will approach it *this* way," not "If only." *If only* it were the great call of disappointment. *Next time* is the great call of faith.

Verse 51: ***"'What do you want me to do for you?' Jesus asked him.* "** I particularly think God is funnier than most of you think He is. If a blind man comes to Jesus and Jesus says, "What do you want me to do for you?" I don't think the guy will say, "I want you to teach me the two-step." It's like, "He's blind! What do you think he wants?" You know what I mean? I think Jesus was trying to point out that you should specifically know what you're going after, but the humor of the moment...

They're bringing a blind man up to him. If he was a man with no legs, do you think the guy would have said, "I want a driver's license"? You know what he wants. He's blind! So, the guy tells straight up. He knows exactly what he wants from God. "I want to see. I can't see. I want to see." Like many of us, this blind man had no vision.

Here's the key: Verse 52: "'Go,' said Jesus, 'your faith has healed you.' Immediately he received his sight and followed Jesus along the road.' I want to tell you this for looking forward and no more looking backward. There's one key component that God requires from every person in this room who names the name of Christ. It takes faith to see. It takes faith to see God. It takes faith ***to see with God.***

So, for those of you stuck in your past, this message brings the past to an end. The past is done. It's over. Let go of it. Don't let the past own you. It's not worth it. You can't do anything about it. Let it go. God is not worried about it. Why are *you* worried about it? Let it go. Whatever happens from this moment forward, that's the way to look.

The bottom line is...be undignified. I'd rather have the corporate church be filled with undignified lunatics who are hungry for God than 5,000 people who come in and go, "We're now going to worship the Lord. Oh, praise you, God. Praise you. Okay. Our ten seconds are up. Let's go home now." I don't want that. Do you want that? Boring. No thank you. Be undignified.

Don't let anything stand between you and God, and don't let anything stop you from getting God's attention. I don't care what you have to do. Do it. Walk forward, and don't look backward. Remember that the whole thing starts on the premise of seeing with faith. Look with faith. The Bible says we walk by faith and not by sight. Amen? All right. Let's pray.

# Chapter 6
# Boat Faith

Matthew, chapter 14, verse 22. The title of this chapter is called *Boat Faith*. We will read the whole text, and then I will go through it line by line and go over the process.

*"Immediately Jesus made the disciples get into the boat and go on ahead of him to the other side, while he dismissed the crowd. After he had dismissed them, he went up on a mountainside by himself to pray. When evening came, he was there alone, but the boat was already a considerable distance from land, buffeted by the waves because the wind was against it.*

*During the fourth watch of the night, Jesus went out to them, walking on the lake. When the disciples saw him walking on the lake, they were terrified. 'It's a ghost,' they said and cried out in fear. But Jesus immediately said to them: 'Take courage! It is I. Don't be afraid.' 'Lord, if it's you,' Peter replied, 'tell me to come to you on the water.' 'Come,' he said.*

*Then Peter got down out of the boat, walked on the water and came toward Jesus. But when he saw the wind, he was afraid and, beginning to sink, cried out, 'Lord, save me!' Immediately, Jesus reached out his hand and caught him. 'You of little faith,' he said, 'why did you doubt?' And when they climbed into the boat, the wind died down. Then those who were in the boat worshiped him, saying, 'Truly you are the Son of God.'"*

Let's look at verse 22. I want us to consider the Christian adventure. In this context, the disciples are with Jesus, and Jesus makes the disciples go into the boat ahead of him and down to a destination. **This represents the Christian adventure**. Do you guys know what's going to happen in fifty minutes? No, you don't. You don't know what's going to happen in five minutes.

Five minutes ago...you're a genius. You can tell everybody all about everything that happened five minutes ago, but five minutes from now, we don't know if there's going to be a big explosion and we're all gone. You have not a clue. This leads us to the Christian adventure, not always knowing what's ahead for us ...that God has in mind. I don't know what tomorrow is going to bring. *All I know is Him who brings tomorrow.*

I have no idea what will happen, but it's an adventure. Sometimes, God will **send us** into situations. Have you ever felt like the Lord sent you into a situation, life lesson, or challenge, and you were like, "Yeah, what am I doing here?" The irony is God sends you there because He has a plan and a purpose. Not that we know what that plan and purpose is all the time. Sometimes it's a mystery. Sometimes we don't know what we're doing. For me, more like most of the time.

We don't have any idea what's going on. We will go somewhere and go, "What am I doing here, Lord?" and the Lord will show us in His time. Sometimes, it's a journey; we must go with the flow. I am the kind of guy, probably like everybody ... I wish all of the ducks were lined up perfectly. Boom, boom, boom. I would know everything that's going to go on, everything that's going to happen.

Whenever I end up lining up the ducks, God pulls out the bigger shotgun and goes *Boom! Boom!* And the ducks fly everywhere, and I'm asking, "What is going on?" I don't know if you've ever gone through that experience where you think you have everything set and know exactly what's happening, and then you wake up the next day, and it's different.

You're like, "Wow! How does that happen?" I'll tell you how it happens. Because it's God's adventure to bring you on, not your adventure to determine. It's the Christian adventure, and you go with the flow. In this case, they were going with the flow. Jesus said, "Go over there." They were like, "All right. Here we go. But I don't know what we're going to do."

I guarantee you if the disciples knew what was about to happen, they would not have gotten into the boat. So Jesus didn't tell them ahead of time. He just said, "Go," and they went.

Look at verse 23. ***"After he had dismissed them*** [the crowd], ***he went up on a mountainside by himself to pray. When evening came, he was there alone..."***

After Jesus sends his disciples out, He goes up to the mountainside to pray. I don't want to elaborate long on this, because I could take 30 minutes on this 15 times in a row. Jesus spent time with the Father through prayer because prayer is the heartbeat of Christianity. If you're going to do all of the things you're going to do, all of the steps, and all this stuff, you really need to spend separate, quiet time with the Lord.

We really need to set aside time alone with God because that is the foundation of our relationship with God... and our immersion into the Word of God itself. Reading the Word of God is God speaking to you, and praying is you speaking to God. That's the essence of a relationship, and the essence of a relationship is at the core of Christianity.

So, if God sends you on a journey, you go wherever the Lord tells you. You don't always get to know what it is, but if you keep praying as the heartbeat, things aren't going to get too bad too fast. However, having said that, let's look at verse 24. *"...but the boat was already a considerable distance from land, buffeted by the waves because the wind was against it."*

I have a question. Who was in the boat? The disciples were in the boat, right? The boat was sent by Jesus. They're in the boat, sent by Jesus, going in the direction of God, and the waves come up, and the wind is contrary.

Look at verse 24 again. *"...but the boat was already a considerable distance from land, buffeted by the waves because the wind was against it."*

These guys are in a boat, and the wind is bashing in on the boat. Here's a really simple question: Are these guys in the will of God? Of course! Jesus told them to get in the boat and go over there. You couldn't get any more in the will of God. It's impossible. Jesus says, "Go in the boat. Go there." They're like, "Okay." So, they're in the perfect will of God, but just because they're in the perfect will of God doesn't mean everything is peachy.

You see, there's a little qualifier there. You think, "If I'm in the will of God, everything has to go smoothly." Well, Jesus was in the will of God, and He was crucified. So, it doesn't always work that way. It doesn't mean everything just goes smoothly. Have you ever gone through buffeting waves and winds that are slightly contrary? You just think, "Oh my gosh!" It's like nothing is going the way you thought it was going to go. That doesn't mean you're not in the will of God.

See, there's a fallacy. "Well, if I'm working perfectly, everything is smooth." Where is that in *this*? "All who live godly in Christ Jesus will suffer persecution." I read *that*. I didn't read, "It's all going to be as smooth as oil if you're in the perfect will of God." It doesn't work that way. The disciples were in the perfect will of God, but things were still tough. Things were hard. This is how God sets it up so He can teach us things.

Verse 25: ***"During the fourth watch of the night, Jesus went out to them, walking on the lake."***

Does anybody else find that bizarre? Is it just me who finds it weird that Jesus is walking on the water? Do you guys not see how bizarre that is? Have you ever gone into a swimming pool? Can you imagine somebody walking across the swimming pool? Can you imagine somebody walking on some big body of water, just walking on top of the water? Like, "What are you doing?"

I'm telling you right now that in the Christian life, there is no such thing as normal. Do you want normal? Don't be a Christian. Stop being a Christian. Quit right now. Get out while you can. Hurry. Because in Christianity, to receive, you have to give. To live, you have to die. To see, you have to believe. All of the formulas work the opposite of what we understand.

Christianity is so bizarre, it works so far out of the realm, you just don't get it. It's like, "Wait a minute. I have to give to receive? I have to die to live? Well, that doesn't seem right." By the world's standards, you're right. It's not. But Christianity is not normal. If you want a normal life, check out now, because you no longer have one. It's gone. It's over. You don't get that chance anymore. There is no normal.

Let's look at verse 26. ***"When the disciples saw him walking on the lake, they were terrified. 'It's a ghost,' they said, and cried out in fear."***

We are too often shocked when God shows up. Jesus comes walking on the water, and you know what they said? "It's a ghost! It's not God; it's a ghost. It's something foreign. It's something weird."

When things happen in a church, spiritual things or spiritual manifestations, people are like, "Oh my gosh! It doesn't seem right. It's not normal. Everybody is not the frozen chosen. I don't know what to do." Let me tell you something. Christianity is not supposed to be about being chosen and frozen and sitting in your blessed assurance and keeping going. That's not what it's supposed to be. Christianity is an adventure where you don't know what God will do.

He shows up, and it's awesome. Instead of being afraid of God, we should thank God that He comes and manifests Himself and does all of these strange things. Instead of freaking out and being shocked that God is doing something, we should be like, "All right. Go, God! Do it. Do more. Do more weird stuff." Why are we so afraid? Because it doesn't fit in our box. We have the Christian box. "This is what Christianity is supposed to be to me." That's great. Who gave you that box? God didn't. Did God give you that box?

We're building up, as you can tell. We're heading in a direction.

Verse 27: ***"But Jesus immediately said to them: 'Take courage! It is I. Don't be afraid.'"***

He says, ***"Take courage."*** Do you know what "Take courage" means? That phrase means "Grab hold of courage." Do you ever feel like you're not feeling the bravest and like you're maybe melting a little inside and may not have the same kind of strength?

Jesus says, "Take courage!" It's like, "Well, how? How do I do that, Jesus?" And He tells you. I want you to look at verse 27 right after "Take courage." ***"It is I."*** Do you know how you take courage? By understanding that "It is I." It's Jesus. It's the I Am. Have you ever heard the expression, "I Am"? Do you know where that comes from? It's a reference in the Old Testament.

Moses said to God, "Well, I'm going to go tell them that you sent me, but who should I say sent me?" God said, "Tell them I Am That I Am." He didn't say, "Tell them 'I was that I was'" or "I will be that I will be." He said, "I Am That I Am." What does that mean in the Hebrew?

It means everything that is necessary or needful at the moment, the I Am is the fulfillment thereof.

God is not the "I will be," and God is not the "I used to be." He's the present tense "I Am." I don't care what your situation is. I don't care how big the waves are. I don't care how big the wind is. The wind can be huge. It can be a huge storm. It's not bigger than the I Am, and the I Am is not disconnected from your life, so He doesn't know what's going on. The I Am is there for you, present, and that's how you take courage. The I Am is whatever we actually (not for the flesh) need for the moment.

Instead of letting things melt us, we should seize strength in God, knowing that He is. Look at the next thing Jesus says. He says, ***"Take courage! It is I. Don't be afraid."*** "You don't understand. It's hard not to be afraid." I understand, but I understand Psalm 23:4: "Though I walk through the valley of the shadow of death, I will fear no evil."

**<u>It's a decision.</u>**

How many of you struggle with fear from time to time? Don't lie to me. People do it all the time. You know what? It's a call. It's a call you make. I know it sounds... "Oh, that's so..." No, it's not. More than a hundred sixty times (not 365) it says, "Fear not." There's a challenge. You don't have to be afraid. But we start down the road of fear, and then the Devil comes along and says, "Yes, you should be afraid. Yes, you should be afraid," and we're like, "Okay." We need to stop doing that. Don't be afraid.

This is the text, the whole point of where we're getting to. I had to go through the whole thing.

Verse 28: ***"'Lord, if it's you,' Peter replied, 'tell me to come to you on the water.' 'Come,' he said."***

I want you to stop and put yourself in the place of Peter, who is in a boat in the middle of the sea where the wind has been tumultuous, and the waves are going up and down. Jesus comes walking on the water, and Peter is like, "All right. If it's you, let me come out to you." Jesus goes, "Come on. The water is fine."

Then the Bible says that Peter got down out of the boat and walked on the water. Jesus was not the only water-walker. Peter did it, too. The call from God, that one moment where Jesus says, "Come on up..." Can you imagine the moment when Peter...goes for it? He's at the boat. He has to get his leg over the boat. He must take his leg over the boat and put it on water. Who in here is not thinking, "See ya!" Who's not thinking that? Unless you have a really good boogie board, I think you know you're going down. Peter just takes the moment and steps out.

God is challenging us not to walk in the status quo. No. Don't. You think, "Well, that's just insane, Dave." Well, then call God nutty, because that's what He's calling us to. He's calling us to get out of the boat. See, the boat is that safety factor we all operate in that keeps everybody A-okay. "We're okay. We can operate within this framework. We make this much. We do this much. It all has to operate within *this*."

God is going, "Get out of the boat. Get out." You're thinking, "Well, that's not logical." Yeah, and this whole Christian thing is? The resurrection from the dead? You think, "That's perfectly logical." What, are you insane? It's so bizarre, and God is going, "Come on! Get out." You're thinking of the status quo. "The boat is right here. I've got my little thing on my... I'm not going nowhere." Well, that's part of the problem. The problem is we don't walk on the water because we don't get out of the boat. You can't do it.

We don't step out. And what a big step it was. I have news for you. I don't know if I could have done that. Do you think you could? I don't know, but I know that Peter, in one moment, said, "All right.

I'll take you on. I'll try this." It's like, "Wow! That's so far-fetched." Yeah, that's God. That's the classic part. That's God. Yeah, that's far out there, outside of the status quo. I love that portion.

It says, ***"Then Peter got down out of the boat, walked on the water and came toward Jesus."*** So, he was doing pretty good. I mean, he was walking on the water. Right? Then what happened? Well, verse 30: ***"But when he saw the wind, he was afraid and, beginning to sink, cried out, 'Lord, save me!'"*** Peter is outside of a boat, walking on water. Okay. Get that one. He's doing it. He's not *trying* it; he's *doing* it, and he's walking toward Jesus.

So, he's got this. "Aha! I'm doing it! This is great!" Then the wind comes, and he does *this*. "Ha, ha, ha, ha, ha...uh-oh." He takes his eyes off of Jesus. Look at what it says in verse 30. ***"But when he saw the wind..."*** He was probably seeing the power of the wind against the water. I am telling you that our eyes affect our faith. This is the key to the whole message and the whole text. Ready? It's in one sentence. ***<u>Where we look determines how we walk</u>***. Period. I'll say it again. Where we look determines how we walk in Christianity.

Had Peter kept his eyes on Jesus and not looked at the wind or the situation around him, he would have just kept on walking right to Jesus. But he took his eyes off the Lord and started looking at his circumstances, and then the circumstances became absurd. Why? Because he's outside of the boat, outside of the box. Suddenly, he's like, "I'm walking on water; this is insane," and down he goes.

This is what we do in our situation. When we're facing a situation, and it's a horrid situation... It's a tough situation. We don't know what to do. The Lord says, "Get out of the boat." We get out of the boat, and we're looking to God. It's like, "We've got faith. We can do this. We can do this." Then we take our eyes off that and start looking at the situation again, and what do we do? We sink, and our faith goes down. We're like, "Uh-oh," and then we're drowning, because that's what happens. Then we're like, "Oh, we're drowning! Oh no!"

You see, where we look determines how we walk. If you look to Jesus and have your sight fixed on Jesus, then the situation will not overpower you. However, if you have your eyes on the situation and are focused on what you're going through, that will drown you. Do you SEE the difference? What you look at determines how you walk. With a fixed vision on Jesus Christ, you can get through any trial in life. Period. Thus says the Lord. I didn't write the book.

Isn't that great? Then you think, "Oh, you know how many times I haven't done that? A trillion." I mean, I start off really good in a situation. You likely start off really good in a situation. You have your eyes on the Lord. "I'm doing it. It's happening." Then some little hiccup comes, and then it's like panic city. I do it all the time, but that's not what the Lord wants me to do. He wants me to keep a fixed vision on him. Where you look determines how you walk.

Verse 31: ***"Immediately Jesus reached out his hand and caught him. 'You of little faith,' he said, 'why did you doubt?'"*** In this case...I want you to catch this...<u>the doubt canceled the faith</u>. It's okay to have a little faith. Jesus would prefer you to have more, but even if you had faith like a mustard seed...pure faith, real, genuine faith...you could do anything. But if you have just a little faith, and then you take that faith and start mixing doubt into it, it eradicates all the faith.

Consequently, doubt eliminates all the power your faith has built. So, you can have this little bit of faith... "I believe God can do this. I believe He can do this." Then you let this doubt come in, and it washes your faith out. There's nothing left. You can't have faith and doubt. That's the whole concept. Even if it's just a little faith, don't mix it with doubt. Mixing it with doubt is what kills the faith.

Fortunately for you and me and all Christians, despite some of our "up and down-ness" and some of our doubting in faith and fighting it and getting out of the boat and drowning and all that stuff, Jesus is always there to rescue us no matter what we're going through. That's what it says in verse 31. ***"Immediately Jesus reached out his hand and caught him..."***

Jesus did not let Peter drown. It was tough. The water was getting up to his neck. He was probably churning away, but Jesus is Mister "Nick of time." He grabbed him and pulled him up. The Bible says in Romans 10:13, "All who call upon the name of the Lord shall be saved." Now, I would prefer not to be saved just before I'm about to drown. I would prefer some prior saving, but I must learn to walk on the water. I have to go through the process.

Then it closes with this. Verse 32: ***"And when they climbed into the boat, the wind died down. Then those who were in the boat worshiped him, saying, 'Truly you are the Son of God.'"*** It is only through Jesus Christ that we can ever find the real peace we need through any and all situations. It is only through Jesus Christ that the peace comes that will put us at some kind of rest and some kind of security. The reason is because Jesus is the Prince of Peace.

So, all that peace we're looking for all of our lives... Everybody is looking for peace of mind, just looking for rest upstairs. All that peace comes through Jesus Christ, and only through Jesus Christ. So, the challenge is this: Get out of the boat. Try to walk on the water. Keep your eyes focused on Jesus. Yeah, I know. It doesn't make sense in so many situations.

I know, but what are you going to do? Let the situation own you, beat you up, diffuse you, take away all joy from life? No. Get out of the boat. Walk on the water. Fix your vision on Jesus Christ. You might get rattled. Jesus will save you. You won't drown. But get your vision focused on Jesus. That will bring you the peace you need. Okay? Let's pray.

# Chapter 7
# God is NOT the Grinch

Do you guys remember the Grinch? He was mean. The Grinch was mean. He was attacking the people. Do you remember what the people were called? The Who's, and they used to live in Whoville. The Who's in Whoville would have a big Christmas pageant (No, this isn't directly Christian. It's a point, being used as a metaphor, so relax).

They would have a big pageant, which would be like a four-day holiday. They would make presents, have feasts, and decorate the trees. Then, every year, they would come around the big Christmas tree, holding hands and singing. Here's some trivia: How many years did the Grinch hear the Who's singing before he decided to take action? Does anybody remember? Oh, that's a good trivia question. Fifty-three years is what the story says.

For 53 years, he had heard it and decided, "No more." So, he decided he was going to steal Christmas. He was mean because he was the kind of person who wasn't happy that somebody else was happy. Do you know what kind of person that is? That's a mean person. That's a person with bitterness and hardness in their heart.

Christians should be the exact opposite of the Grinch in every case. In fact, if we're following Scripture, which says, "Look not every man on his own things, but also on the things of others," our biggest passion should be the success of others because Jesus' biggest compassion was everybody else doing better.

He had to fulfill his mission. He did it so everybody could spend eternity with God, but He wanted everybody to do better. That's Christian. Not happy that people are doing well? Not happy and wanting to stop people from being able to do well?  Not Christian. Much more like the Grinch.

Let's look at our passage, 1 Kings, chapter 18. We are going to be reading from verse 20. It's a wonderful portion that many of you know well. After this Old Testament section, we will go through seven New Testament verses, and then we will be done. First Kings 18, starting in verse 20:

*"So Ahab sent word throughout all Israel and assembled the prophets on Mount Carmel. Elijah went before the people and said, 'How long will you waver between two opinions? If the Lord is God, follow him; but if Baal is God, follow him.' But the people said nothing. Then Elijah said to them, 'I am the only one of the Lord's prophets left, but Baal has four hundred and fifty prophets.*

*Get two bulls for us. Let them choose one for themselves and let them cut it into pieces and put it on the wood but not set fire to it. I will prepare the other bull and put it on the wood but not set fire to it. Then you call on the name of your god, and I will call on the name of the Lord. The god who answers by fire—he is God.' Then all the people said, 'What you say is good.'"*

So that you know, you have the God of Israel and Baal. In this case, Baal is Hadad, the storm god, the god who's in charge of fire, wind, and lightning. This is the god who would be in charge of fire falling from heaven. This was the Baal that was specifically being referred to.

Elijah issues a challenge. "Hey, I've got it. Let's have a straight-out contest. Straight up, no messing around. I take a bull. You take a bull. You call. I call. Whichever one gets the sacrifice taken, that one has the real God." That's straight up. Nothing is weird about that. Here we go. Verse 25:

*"Elijah said to the prophets of Baal, 'Choose one of the bulls and prepare it first, since there are so many of you. Call on the name of your god, but do not light the fire.' So they took the bull given them and prepared it. Then they called on the name of Baal from morning till noon. 'O Baal, answer us!' they shouted. But there was no response; no one answered. And they danced around the altar they had made."*

I'd like you to get the picture without me having to actually show you the picture. They're all hanging around, and it's morning till noon, roughly about 9:00 a.m. to 12:00 p.m., for at least three hours, and they're dancing around this bull. "O Baal, answer!" They're dancing around the bull.

Verse 27: *"At noon Elijah began to taunt them. 'Shout louder!' he said. 'Surely he is a god! Perhaps he is deep in thought, or busy, or traveling. Maybe he is sleeping and must be awakened.'"* Now, for those who are not familiar with the Hebrew... (I was born and raised Jewish and became a Christian if that helps some of you.)The word *busy* there is not what you think it means. It's that *other* than what you think it means. "I'll be back in just a few moments. I'm going to be busy." That's what that means.

In Hebrew, it means he's on the toilet. "Maybe he's on the toilet." This is how Elijah is taunting these guys. "Maybe he's sleeping. Maybe he's in the john. Maybe he's doing *this*. Maybe he's traveling. Surely your god can respond at some point." Now, if you're one of the people of Baal, I think at this point your level of pride is going pretty low because you're being taunted literally in relationship to the god you "believe in."

*"'Shout louder!' he said. 'Surely he is a god! Perhaps he is deep in thought, or busy, or traveling. Maybe he is sleeping and must be awakened.' So they shouted louder and slashed themselves with swords and spears, as was their custom until their blood flowed."* Sounds like a fanatic kind of group. *"Midday passed, and they continued their frantic prophesying until the time for the evening sacrifice. But there was no response, no one answered, no one paid attention."* So, they went from 9:00 to 5:00, shouting, dancing, beating themselves. Verse 30:

*"Then Elijah said to all the people, 'Come here to me.' They came to him, and he repaired the altar of the Lord, which was in ruins. Elijah took twelve stones, one for each of the tribes descended from Jacob, to whom the word of the Lord had come, saying, 'Your name shall be Israel.' With the stones he built an altar in the name of the Lord, and he dug a trench around it large enough to hold two seahs of seed.*

*He arranged the wood, cut the bull into pieces and laid it on the wood. Then he said to them, 'Fill four large jars with water and pour it on the offering and on the wood.' 'Do it again,' he said, and they did it again. 'Do it a third time,' he ordered, and they did it the third time. The water ran down around the altar and even filled the trench.*

*At the time of sacrifice, the prophet Elijah stepped forward and prayed: 'O Lord, God of Abraham, Isaac and Israel, let it be known today that you are God in Israel and that I am your servant and have done all these things at your command.*

*Answer me, O Lord, answer me, so these people will know that you, O Lord, are God, and that you are turning their hearts back again.'*

*Then the fire of the Lord fell and burned up the sacrifice, the wood, the stones and the soil, and also licked up the water in the trench. When all the people saw this, they fell prostrate and cried, 'The Lord—He is God! The Lord—He is God!'"*

Okay. Two very interesting contrasting pictures. The prophets of Baal are beating themselves, dancing, crying, screaming, and yelling, trying to get the attention of their god, but there is no response. Elijah gets up and speaks for one minute and 20 seconds, if he took his time and spoke very slowly, and in a minute and 20 seconds, *Bammo!* Fire comes from heaven. Are you seeing a contrast here?

What's my point? Listen. It's simple. We do not have to dance for the Almighty to respond to us. You do not have to dance. You don't have to do *this*. You don't have to do *this*. You don't have to bang your head on the ground. You don't have to do any of those things for God to answer you. We do not have to cut ourselves for God to hear us. We do not have to stick our hands in a blender. We do not have to chop off a finger. None of those things are required. Do you want to know why none of those things are required?

You think, "Dave, you're slightly upset again." No, I'm not. I'm just trying to explain that God is not into performance orientation. "How dare you say that?" I didn't say it. Romans, chapter 5. Performance orientation. "Do this correctly, and I will give you a dollar. Do this correctly, and I will give you a piece of candy. Do this as I have told you to, and I will reward you. I will reward your behavior strictly based on the fact that you perform your behavior based on the context that I want you to perform your behavior."

We have assumed that God operates in this principle, and I want to demonstrate how ridiculous that is in a second, but let us talk about performance orientation growing up. All of us had really good parents, and I am a parent and am really good, at implementing performance orientation life. "Do *this*; get *that*. Don't do *this*; get a swat on the butt. Do *this*; get *that*. Don't do *this*; no Nintendo. Do *this*. Don't do *that*."

I mean, listen to all of the things we do. I want one person here to tell me you don't operate that way, and you'll be getting an hour-long message I preached 20 years ago about ***"Thou shalt not bear false witness,"*** because that is how we function an enormous amount of time. We don't understand unconditional love; we understand performance. If we're not performing to the perfect standard, we're not perfect and don't qualify.

That, my friends, is not God. You think, "Well, no, there's a lot in there that says it's that way, Dave." Nope. It starts off when God gives you a blank slate, and He might try to teach you different principles, but his underlying theme is unconditional love, unchangeable. Romans 5:8 proves this. You cannot argue with Scripture. Romans 5:8: ***"But God demonstrates his own love for us in this: while we were still sinners, Christ died for us."***

What exactly did we do in our performance orientation to deserve this? Nothing. What could you have done? Nothing. Impossible. You see, you can't turn around and say, "Well, God died for us because He loved us while we were still sinners." If you don't see that, I quit. The bottom line is the basis of God's principle of operation is unconditional love. Now, there is a reward system, but the foundation of everything God does with his kids is love, love, love.

God could have wiped out the planet, but He was committed to His love for the sinful people that we are. There's no one in this room who hasn't stuck their hand high up to heaven and said, "I'm not going to listen to what you say," and God is still there. God didn't take the moment and judge you according to your sin, or we'd all be a heap of ashes. We'd be dead. In the mercy of God, He watches out for us.

I will share something that happened to me with you, and then we will blitz through the rest of it. I told this in the Bible study, but I want to tell the other part. I was a young Christian. I was on fire for the Lord, witnessing down where the prostitutes were and having the pimps pull their guns. It was a great experience.

I'm on fire for the Lord, so I decided it was time for my first big fast. Why was it time for my first big fast? Because somebody told me, "Well, truly spiritual Christians all fast." I'm like, "Well, that's it. I've got to do it." Of course, my motivation was pride. I decided I would fast, so I had to pick a number. "Well, how long do people fast for? A day." I'm thinking, "I can do a day. Two days. That's a good one. Three days. Five days. I'm going to fast for five days." (I could use that again now, but that's beside the point.)

"I'm going to fast five days. I'm not going to eat anything for five days. I will show the Lord I am so right there for him. I'm going to do it perfectly." So, day one goes by, and it's not really a problem. You know, one day. Day two comes by. It's getting a little worse, because on the television every so often, there are commercials for fast food that I don't normally think are that good, but all of a sudden, on my second day, they have this new air about them that maybe makes them more interesting.

Day three goes by, and you never notice how many restaurants are in Phoenix, Arizona, until you're driving in Phoenix, Arizona, and you notice all the restaurants. I'm hungry, thinking, "Yeah, I'd eat there." You know, Bob's Chinese Taco and Irish Burrito Shop. "Oh, that sounds good." You know, whatever it is, I'm ready for it. So, I get to day four and think, "I can do this." I'm spending a lot of time praying and in the Word, but I'm doing it alone.

I get to day four and 22 to 23 hours. I only have a couple of hours left. I feel my stomach is falling. I feel like I've lost it. We lived in Fairfield Greens. So, I walk out. I'm there with my brother in a room. I come out to the little living room and get down on my hands and knees. I'm like, "Lord, I'm trying to seek after you. I really love you. I'm trying to prove," and so on and so forth.

Then I walk by the kitchen. We have a small kitchen. I mean, it's small. When I say "small," it's like *this*. What's on the kitchen counter is a loaf of bread. I go, "Bread. Bread. Oh, bread. That kind of sounds good, bread. Bread ...it sounds like I'd like a piece of bread, even though I only needed to wait a few hours. But bread. Oh, bread. Bread, butter...bread and butter."

So, three minutes later, after those two slices were consumed in a one-second moment (I think I ate it like an Oreo cookie), I get down on my hands and knees, and then I'm overwhelmed with guilt. I feel like, "I blew it! I blew it for God. I just had a couple of hours to go and blew it. God is going to be upset with me." I open my *Thompson Chain-Reference Bible*, the King James Version, to Isaiah 58 at the top (it should still be there), and it says, "The fast which God accepteth..." I thought, "Oh, the Lord has had mercy."

I'm feeling a lot better, so I go to bed, and I'm half happy, half sad. I wake up and go out with my partner the next day. While he's driving and I'm in the car, it's the first time God ever speaks to me where He interrupts my thoughts. Not where an idea comes in, but I'm actually thinking about something, and it's like everything gets put on hold and God has a message, and here it is. I'd never heard this before. I've only heard this four or five times in my Christian walk after 45 years.

He told me five words, and I am telling you, I have tried to follow those five words every day. I believe that next to Scripture, it is the most important thing I've ever encountered. God said, "You cannot merit my love." I thought, "I cannot merit your love." I kept thinking, "Well, why not? I should be able to earn everything else." I was so far gone. I so far didn't get it. "You cannot merit my love."

I was like, "But I've got to do something!" Doesn't everybody feel that way? You've got to do something. No, you cannot merit his love. You cannot merit God's love. Sorry. It's like, "Well, well..." No. You can fast for 50 years. You're not going to merit the love of God. It doesn't matter. You could be the most spiritual person in the world. You could be the coolest person in the world. You could be the most awesome everything in the universe. You cannot merit God's love. God loves you because God is love. You can't merit that love. He just gives it.

So, being devastated from that moment, but growing quickly, understanding how stupid I could be...incredible...it dawned on me that I was having a problem up here between these enormous antennas. I was having a real problem. Do you know what my problem was? I had false images...have, had, and probably will have...of God. I have the wrong picture of God in my head.

Turn to Matthew, chapter 7. Here's the key. I have false images of God that are in my mind (and the false images that are in my mind have to do probably with people in my past or whatever the case may be) that God is stingy and cheap, that maybe he's working on approved credit only. There are all of these qualifiers. But here's what God has to say. Matthew 7:7:

*"Ask, and it will be given to you; seek, and you will find; knock, and the door will be opened to you. For everyone who asks receives; He who seeks finds; and to him who knocks, the door will be opened. Which of you, if his son asks for bread, will*

*give him a stone? Or if he asks for a fish, will give him a snake? If you, then, though you are evil, know how to give good gifts to your children, how much more will your Father in heaven give good gifts to those who ask him!"*

If you have anything in your mind when you're praying other than this passage, you are missing who God is by a country mile. The Bible says in Ephesians, ***"Now unto him that is able to do exceeding abundantly above all that we ask or think..."*** There is so much kindness, generosity, passion, mercy, and love in God that every time we pray, we must remove the cheap, stingy picture that steps in there, thinking, "Well, maybe God will give it to me, maybe He won't. Maybe He will, maybe He won't. I don't know."

Instead, maybe we should start believing that God is a generous God. Do you ever say to yourself, "God is generous"? He *is* generous. Let's just settle this once and for all. Simple issue. The issue must be resolved, and the only thing you must remember the rest of the day is this. Every time you pray, you must settle *this* issue: <u>Is God a giver or the Grinch</u>? Before you pray, you must answer that question. **Is God a giver, or is God the Grinch?**

Let's look to Romans 8:32. <u>Is God a giver or the Grinch?</u> ***"He who did not spare his own Son, but gave him up for us all—how will he not also, along with him, graciously give us all things?"*** Not only is God, not the Grinch, but he is Mister Generous. You have to think of God as Mister Generous, Mister Giver, anything but the Grinch, every time you pray, you must remember and believe, ***"Without faith, it's impossible to please God, for those who come to God must believe that he is and a rewarder of those who seek him."*** It's that simple.

So, God is not the Grinch. He's not tight, stingy, or mean. He's not like any human parent you know anywhere. He's not like your dad, your mom, or any of your parents. God is gracious and generous and a giver. You can come to Him anytime, anywhere, and petition him, and He is a responder, a giver, and generous.

We'll close with Luke 12:32. This is the bottom line. Ready? I'm going to say this really simply. The bottom line is we need to stop being stupid and get to know God's heart. Here's God's heart. Luke 12:32: ***"Do not be afraid, little flock, for your Father has been pleased to give you the kingdom."***

It is the pleasure of God to help you and give to you. It's his pleasure. He enjoys it. So, when you're praying, think of that. Don't think, "Will I get this from Him or not? Can I slide this one by? Do you think you could sneak me one behind the back? Come on." God is Mister Generous. Stop thinking he's Mister Stingy, because according to your faith, so be it. God is not the Grinch at all. He loves to give. Let's pray.

# Chapter 8
# By Him...We Win

By Him, we win. Winner, winner, chicken dinner. "Winner? What do you mean, winner?" All right. Let me help you out. Tell me if you can relate to this portion of Scripture. It's one of my favorites, and one of my friends from my past, who became a Christian later in his life... This is *his* favorite portion of Scripture. Every time I read it, I think of him, because he has talked to me about it at length. Mark 9:14-24. I'll go through it quickly, but the point is the point, so let's follow.

*"When they came to the other disciples, they saw a large crowd around them and the teachers of the law arguing with them. As soon as all the people saw Jesus, they were overwhelmed with wonder and ran to greet him. 'What are you arguing with them about?' he asked. A man in the crowd answered, 'Teacher, I brought you my son, who is possessed by a spirit that has robbed him of speech. Whenever it seizes him, it throws him to the ground. He foams at the mouth, gnashes his teeth and becomes rigid. I asked your disciples to drive out the spirit, but they could not.'*

*'O unbelieving generation,' Jesus replied, 'how long shall I stay with you? How long shall I put up with you? Bring the boy to me.' So they brought him. When the spirit saw Jesus, it immediately threw the boy into a convulsion. He fell to the ground and rolled around, foaming at the mouth. Jesus asked the boy's father, 'How long has he been like this?'*

*'From childhood,' he answered. 'It has often thrown him into fire or water to kill him. But if you can do anything, take pity on us and help us.' '"If you can"?' said Jesus. 'Everything is possible for him who believes.' Immediately the boy's father exclaimed, 'I do believe; help me overcome my unbelief!'"*

What a portion. You know the story. You've heard it before, but the real key is understanding that Jesus tells him... This is going to be fantastic. We will demonstrate something, and it's possible if the guy will believe. The guy says the most honest thing. I love these honest statements in Scripture. He says, "I do believe. I have a measure of faith. I do, but I have unbelief, too, and I need You to help me overcome that."

Do you know what's great about this portion? In Jesus you win, but the thing that keeps us from that win is that unbelief, that doubt, that distrust. That's what keeps us away. Jesus says in Matthew 21:21, *"I tell you the truth, if you have faith and do not doubt, not only can you do what was done to the fig tree, but also you can say to this mountain, 'Go, throw yourself into the sea,' and it will be done."*

In Matthew 17:20, he says, *"Because you have so little faith. I tell you the truth, if you have faith as small as a mustard seed, you can say to this mountain, 'Move from here to there' and it will move. Nothing will be impossible for you."* Jesus is telling people, "Faith is the ticket," and the guy is so honest. He says, "You know what? I only have a little faith."

In faith, we get to do tremendous things with God. It's faith that pleases God. We get to partner with God. We get to see miraculous things happen with God. We get to see prayers answered by the Lord. The Lord does all of this, but He has chosen the operation of faith to do it. The guy says, "I have a little bit of that faith, but, Jesus, help me overcome my unbelief." He's acknowledging that in his compartment, there is faith, and there is doubt.

Here's what you have to understand. This will be the easiest way to keep it if you can understand it. If you simply can understand that faith moves things, that faith is in one cup in your life and doubt is in another, and that if you have two ounces of faith and two ounces of doubt, nothing is getting done. You just canceled them out.

It's not as though you must have two straight fluid ounces of faith. You only need a mustard seed, but that mustard seed must be pure, real, and genuine. If you have doubt, if you have unbelief that's on an equal plane to your faith, nothing will get done because you're canceling out the faith.

People are like, "No, no! That's ridiculous." Really? That's 18 times in Matthew, Mark, Luke, and John. Ridiculous? That's exactly what the Scripture teaches. When you allow doubt to enter into the cup, it's almost like you put one kind of liquid and another kind of liquid, and when you put them together, they become a third liquid, and it ruins everything. It can happen with soda and, maybe, Nestle Quik. If you put in the same amounts in a cup, it will be like, "Bleh!" You can't drink that. What's that?

Well, that's what you do to your faith. You're dropping Nestle Quik into a Coke. That doesn't work. Then it becomes unusable. We need to get away from that. We need to have genuine faith, that's real, that's alone...even just a mustard seed, but it has to be beyond the unbelief and the doubt. So, let's look at that process, as Scripture defines it, because sometimes we need help, and ***faith comes by hearing and hearing by the Word of God.***

By Jesus, we win. If you're unsure if there's victory in Jesus, we will show Scriptures that declare that. That is not the problem. The problem is not whether there is victory in Jesus Christ. That is really not the problem for the Christian. The problem for the Christian seems to be whether we believe it, not whether it is so or not.

One of the things you get to do in theology is you get to talk about ex nihilo and different things like this. It doesn't matter whether human beings believe something or not. If God declared it, it's that way whether people agree with it or not. It's not a relevant point. Well, it's irrelevant if you don't think in Jesus you win. In Jesus, you win. The problem is if you don't believe it, you'll never access it. It doesn't really matter.

This is a reality that goes beyond human understanding. You get into the philosophy of humanity. It's fantastic that people think, "Well, in my universe, it's *this*. In my universe, it's *that*." Great. If every human being rejected God, fine. It doesn't change the reality of God in His existence that people give approval or disapproval.

It's like, "Well, no, that's bad, because then God wouldn't be winning the war of PR." It doesn't matter. God will exist, keep going, be defined, and prevail regardless of what people approve of or don't approve of. It doesn't matter. Again, in Jesus Christ, you have victory. Now, whether you access that victory or not... That is something you work on in the Lord.

If you don't believe it, you'll have to get over that, just like Mark in chapter 9, the guy with the son who had the spirit. You're going to have to overcome the unbelief. If you need help doing it, you need to ask God. "You know what? I don't have pure, genuine faith. I do have a lot of unbelief. I need some help." I don't think there's anything weird or bizarre about that.

I think many saints... They do not ask for a sign for the Messiah, but many people of God ask for Him to give them an affirmation. Gideon asked for it. Abraham... "How do I know?" There are many times that has happened. So, here's what I'm trying to lay out before you. In Jesus Christ, there's victory.

Second Corinthians 2:14 says, ***"But thanks be to God, who always leads us as captives in Christ's triumphal procession..."*** In other words, Jesus is marching down the street. He's marching in a triumph parade, and you're a part of the parade. You're a part of that process. You're a part of that procession. We need to get that. Now, I know it gets hard. I want to use this psalm to determine where we're going with this. Psalm 30:4-12:

***"Sing the praises of the Lord, you his faithful people; praise his holy name. For his anger lasts only a moment, but his favor lasts a lifetime; weeping may stay for the night, but rejoicing comes in the morning. When I felt secure, I said, 'I will never be shaken.' Lord, when you favored me, you made my royal mountain stand firm; but when you hid your face, I was dismayed.***

***To you, Lord, I called; to the Lord, I cried for mercy: 'What is gained if I am silenced, if I go down to the pit? Will the dust praise you? Will it proclaim your faithfulness? Hear, Lord, and be merciful to me; Lord, be my help.' You turned my wailing into dancing; you removed my sackcloth and clothed me with joy, that my heart may sing your praises and not be silent. Lord my God, I will praise you forever."***

This is a fantastic portion of Scripture. If you don't know Psalm 30, you need to read it one, two, three...ten times. Really, what He's saying is that even if it's hard, because of Jesus Christ, if you believe, it may be Friday, but Sunday is coming. Do you know what that phrase means? Jesus Christ was crucified on a Friday and resurrected on a Sunday.

So, it may be Friday, and you might feel like it's Friday. You might feel like it's dark and down. You might have a little, itty, bitty faith, but you say, "Lord, I need to have more faith. Help me to overcome my unbelief. Help me to remove my doubt," and you will move from the position of understanding that it's Friday, but Sunday is coming. The crucifixion is there, but the resurrection is en route.

We need to stop sitting there and stewing on the Friday and start living on the Sunday. Hey, Jesus went through a lot, but he got up. One of the contentious areas between Evangelicals and Catholic believers is the cross. A lot of Catholic believers, more so than evangelicals, have Jesus on the cross. The evangelicals say, "He's off that thing. He's not on there."

That is the whole point of the faith. Right? It's not telling the story without the proper ending. He rose from the dead. That is the point. I mean, apart from that, there is no faith. "It's Christian existentialism." There is no such thing. That's a lie. You either believe He resurrected, or you don't. So, the idea is to understand that that doubt pulls you into this place where you sit on Friday and don't see Sunday coming.

If you want to know if you're the only one who goes through it, the disciples went through it. Jesus resurrected. They saw Jesus. And what does the Scripture say? "Some doubted." They saw Him! "Oh, no. I don't think that's really Him. Is it Him? Maybe it's him." I can guarantee you that after Acts 2:4, they knew it was Him. It might be Friday, but Sunday is coming. In Him, we have this victory.

In Jesus Christ, we win, but many of us have a hard time accessing that "winnability." By win, we mean prevail. By win, we mean exactly what Jesus said, you know, speaking unto the mountain. In that situation, in that hyperbole, He's talking about utilizing faith to encounter a circumstance. That's it. There's nothing more.

If you don't use that faith, you won't see that victory the way you need to. How many times throughout Matthew, Mark, Luke, and John... There's nothing impossible to you if you are engaged and connected with the King and if you are operating in that faith. Then we see in Mark 9 that a gentleman whose son had a demonic spirit problem had faith. He had a genuine faith. He even said, "I believe." It's just that he was having a hard time overcoming his unbelief.

I think that is the struggle many of us go through. We have two ounces of faith and two ounces of doubt. You put those together, and you have nothing. They're canceling each other out. I guess if you said it this way... There would be nothing if you took two ounces of fire and two ounces of water and put them together in one thing. It wouldn't be pure water, and it wouldn't be fire. It's like, "Oops!" You'd have ash water, I guess. I'm just saying it doesn't work.

So, we need to have a purity that goes with it. Then we talked about how some of us don't recognize that there is this triumphal procession. Second Corinthians 2:14 is not in there by accident. It's not out of context to say that Jesus leads us into victorious places. That's exactly what He does. Not just in one circumstance but, ultimately, in every circumstance, we know that God is weaving it together for good; therefore, in every circumstance, we are victorious just by the conclusion of the Scripture.

Typically, we'll go into Romans 8:28 and examine that. I want to do something a little different. I want to examine the Scriptures, but I want to examine the Scriptures **after** Romans 8:28 because we spend so much time talking about 8:28. You know, *"**All things work together for good to them that love God, to them that are called*** *according to his purpose."* So, we believe God works things together for good.

The New American Standard Bible says God **_causes_** all things to work together for good. Another version says we **_know_** in all things God works together for good. If you're not getting the gist of the message, you're trying to dig down too deep to catch what God is saying. "It's going to turn good. Bad turns rad. Give me some time." That's what it is. But I want to look at the post verses, Romans 8:31-37. We should know these verses. Most of us do know these.

*"What, then, shall we say in response to these things? If God is for us, who can be against us? He who did not spare his own Son but gave him up for us all—how will he not also graciously give us all things along with him, hardship, persecution, famine, nakedness, danger, or sword?"* Verse 37: *"No, in all these things we are more than conquerors through him who loved us."*

You can't go into Scripture and find too many verses like these seven verses that state time and time again, "You win in Jesus. In Jesus, you win." Look at the first portion, verse 31: *"What, then, shall we say in response to these things? If God is for us, who can be against us?"* If God is for you, then whoever is against you... Who cares?

"The Devil is against me." You know, when the Devil was thrown out of heaven, as we see in Revelation, chapter 12, God didn't do it. He had Michael the Archangel do it. He didn't even get up. "You take care of it. I'm going to sit here." You have to understand. This isn't really that equal war between Satan and God. Oh, it's warfare between the kingdom of light and the kingdom of darkness, but it is a concluded war. It's already done.

Again, when Satan gets tossed, it's not God. God just has Michael, the Archangel, do it. If Michael the Archangel can throw Satan out of heaven, how much more power does God have than Satan? Okay. Got it. So, it's like, "If God is for us, who can be against us?" Who cares? That's exactly what it's trying to say.

Then along those lines, for those who may think God is a little stingy, verse 32: ***"He who did not spare his own Son, but gave him up for us all—how will he not also, along with him, graciously give us all things?"*** It's like, "Okay. Cool." This is where you get into the heart of it. "I know. But, Dave, I want to have victory in my life. I want to walk in that victory." Yeah, well, that is where Romans 8:37 comes into play.

It gives you a list in verse 35. It discusses trouble, hardship, persecution, famine, nakedness, danger, and the sword. Have you ever had trouble? Have you ever had hardship? Well, guess what? Trouble and hardship all go to the same verse, verse 37. What does verse 37 say? "In all these things (we just named), we are more than conquerors."

You don't just win in Him. Can I say this in a wonderful way? You *really* win in Him. I mean, really, really, really. You're thinking, "Well, 'More than conquerors...' That only means in salvation." I agree with you that it means salvation, first and foremost, always, but it says two verses earlier, "Trouble, hardship, persecution, famine, nakedness, danger, and sword."

It lists seven things, two of which are *trouble* and *hardship*, equating to anything. But it doesn't matter because in all things and all those things, in Jesus, we're more than prevailing. Now, does that mean because you're more than a conqueror in Jesus, The Father will fix your bank account? No. That's not what it means. It doesn't mean God is a genie who pulls out cash and throws it at you. God is not an ATM machine.

God guarantees you that if you pursue Him, if you seek Him. If you make the kingdom of God your passion and priority and seek His righteousness, which is the righteousness *from* God and *of* God, you won't have to be concerned about what you eat, drink, or wear. You won't have to be concerned about the basics. God will take care of it.

If you want to pierce yourself through with many sorrows because you want to create a life of luxury on this planet, that's your choice, but God's promise is He will take care of you at the core. There will be nothing you will ever have to be concerned about. He will make sure your mission is fulfilled, and He'll be with you every step of the way. As you go through each and every trial, He will help you overcome, not just squeeze by. A few too many Christians only think they will just barely squeeze by.

I appreciate that Peter was doing great and walking on the water, but after he took his eyes off of Jesus, he sank and started to go down, but Jesus was right there and picked him right back up, an arm's length away. That's how close the Lord is for you and me. In everything we go through, we win. There's a winning that takes place. I'm not going to go down the Donald Trump line. "Winning, winning, winning." Okay, I did.

Okay. That's all cute, but I'm talking about eternally. I'm talking about it currently. The King of the universe, through His Son Jesus Christ, has enabled you to prevail as not just a conqueror but *more* than a conqueror, *above* just conquering, because if God and you are walking together, nothing can stop you. That's it. So walk with God, and you'll be in the majority because God is the majority.

It's a reality check to look at 2 Corinthians 2:14 and understand that in Jesus Christ, there is a triumphal procession. We understand there's a struggle in that process. Mark, in chapter 9, makes it clear. The father of the young boy who had a demonic spirit said, "You know, I believe. Help me overcome my unbelief." He did acknowledge, and it was, I think, a wonderful thing in Scripture. He said, "You know, I do have a little bit of faith, but I've got doubt, and it's killing it."

That's exactly what it is. Two ounces of doubt, two ounces of faith. Mix them together, and you have nothing. That's what you have...nothing. No plus, no minus...zero. Jesus said you just need a mustard seed. That'd change everything. So, you need to have more faith going than you have doubt operating. You have to get rid of that doubt. That's the thing we need to come before the Lord in.

We understand as you look at Romans 8:28... Things work together for good. You look at verses 31-37 and read that we have more. I don't know how to say this. I'm not sure if I can say this well enough. We are more than conquerors. For those of you who think of Michael Moore, just think how large he is. He's more than an average person. See? That's how you might think of it. It's more.

My point in that is for you to understand... Hey, in Christ, you can do this. "I can do all things through Christ who strengthens me." I'm going to wind this down with a cool story. This little segment is called *Facing Giants*. Let's look at the passage from which we pull all of this. It says this in 1 Samuel:

*"Meanwhile, the Philistine, with his shield-bearer in front of him, kept coming closer to David. He looked David over and saw that he was little more than a boy, glowing with health and handsome, and he despised him. He said to David, 'Am I a dog, that you come at me with sticks?' And the Philistine cursed David by his gods. 'Come here,' he said, 'and I'll give your flesh to the birds and the wild animals!'*

*David said to the Philistine, 'You come against me with sword and spear and javelin, but I come against you in the name of the Lord Almighty, the God of the armies of Israel, whom you have defied. This day, the Lord will deliver you into my hands, and I'll strike you down and cut off your head.*

*This very day, I will give the carcasses of the Philistine army to the birds and the wild animals, and the whole world will know that there is a God in Israel. All those gathered here will know that it is not by sword or spear that the Lord saves; for the battle is the Lord's, and he will give all of you into our hands.'*

*As the Philistine moved closer to attack him, David ran quickly toward the battle line to meet him. Reaching into his bag and taking out a stone, he slung it and struck the Philistine on the forehead. The stone sank into his forehead, and he fell facedown on the ground. So David triumphed over the Philistine with a sling and a stone; without a sword in his hand he struck down the Philistine and killed him."*

That's what you and I have to do against these giants we face that try to speak doubt and take away the victory that was in the Lord. Look at Goliath, 9'2" to 9'6", most likely 9'6". That's just a few inches underneath the rim on a basketball court. Consider how big that guy was, and David just says, "Look. You're coming at me with the sword. You're coming at me with javelin. You're coming at me with the spear. I'm coming against you in the name of the Lord, and you're going down."

That is believing and operating in faith that victory comes in connection with God. For those of you who are going, "Well, this is far-fetched..." Oh, I didn't realize King David was far-fetched. I thought he was an example for us, and we were part of that lineage that came through him, as Jesus came through him, spoke unto us, and gave us eternal life. I thought we were all connected to Abraham and David.

David was the one who looked at this big giant and said, "No way, man. I'm doing this in God, and I'm doing this now. I'm taking you down. Your army will go bye-bye, and you'll discover what victory is."

Why can't Christians live like that? How can that be right for him and wrong for us? How could it be wrong to have passages like 1 Corinthians 15:57 that say, "Thanks be unto God. He always gives us victory through our Lord Jesus Christ"?

That's not wrong. What's wrong is that we don't use it. What's wrong is that we don't believe it. What's wrong is that we operate in an unbelieving position, that we operate in unbelief and in doubt with a God who has demonstrated himself ten thousand times faithful. What's wrong is that we don't believe that or hold that.

You're going to face whatever you're going to face. Cut the giant's head off with faith. You can do this through Christ. He has already made that clear. We just have to decide to operate the way God has set before us. That example of King David is an example for us to live by. You look at your Goliath and say, "No way. You are not bigger than my God." You'll see the victory because the victory is in Jesus. Let's pray.

# Chapter 9
# Are The Sails Up?

The title of this chapter is, *Are the Sails Up?* Luke, chapter 5. We will go from verses 1 to 11. We will review the whole portion, then go back and exposit it verse (or verses) by verse, starting with verse 1.

*"One day as Jesus was standing by the Lake of Gennesaret, with the people crowding around him and listening to the word of God, he saw at the water's edge two boats, left there by the fishermen, who were washing their nets. He got into one of the boats, the one belonging to Simon, and asked him to put out a little from shore. Then he sat down and taught the people from the boat.*

*When he had finished speaking, he said to Simon, 'Put out into deep water, and let down the nets for a catch.' Simon answered, 'Master, we've worked hard all night and haven't caught anything. But because you say so, I will let down the nets.' When they had done so, they caught such a large number of fish that their nets began to break. So they signaled their partners in the other boat to come and help them, and they came and filled both boats so full that they began to sink.*

***When Simon Peter saw this, he fell at Jesus' knees and said, 'Go away from me, Lord; I am a sinful man!' For he and all his companions were astonished at the catch of fish they had taken, and so were James and John, the sons of Zebedee, Simon's partners. Then Jesus said to Simon, 'Don't be afraid; from now on you will catch men.' So they pulled their boats up on shore, left everything and followed him.*"** Let's pray.

Verses 1-3, a little intro stuff. Jesus was, technically, at the *Sea of Galilee.* The Sea of Galilee is an important spot in the history and ministry of Christ because it's a place where some of the early miracles of Jesus took place, a place that was kind of like a launching pad for His ministry. This is also a place where He chose His disciples. This is where He selected them. So, this place has some "sentimental" value with the Lord as He's moving about on the planet and doing things.

The reason, specifically, that He taught in this particular location is because the Sea of Galilee was set up kind of like a cove. There were so many people who wanted to hear what Jesus had to say, and they really didn't have amplification systems back then, so Jesus used the cove as an instant amphitheater so He could go out in the boats and reach everybody talking without having to scream, like most of us moronic pastors who teach. He could just speak it, and the waters would help the volume go along, and He could reach hundreds and thousands of people.

So, here's Jesus. He's hanging out there. He's in Peter's boat. He's in the water. He's teaching everybody. He's done with his teaching, then turns and talks to Peter. Verse 4: "***When he had finished speaking, he said to Simon, 'Put out into deep water, and let down the nets for a catch.'*"** Now, who is this who is speaking to Peter? Jesus. And who is Jesus? He's the Son of the living God. This isn't some guy who's going around just trying to make a living.

Who told Peter? Jesus. This is the key. Jesus is telling Peter, "Hey, put your net out there. You're going to catch something." This is God communicating to man. I want you to know this is the heart of God for us, as Christians. God wants his people to be an expectant people. So, what Jesus tells Peter is, "Hey, man. Put your net out there in the water. You're going to get some fish. Hey, be expectant. You're going to catch something." I want you to turn to Mark, chapter 11, verse 20.

*"In the morning, they saw the fig tree withered from the roots as they went along. Peter remembered and said to Jesus, 'Rabbi, look! The fig tree you cursed has withered!' 'Have faith in God,' Jesus answered. 'I tell you the truth, if anyone says to this mountain, "Go, throw yourself into the sea," and does not doubt in his heart but believes that what he says will happen, it will be done for him. Therefore I tell you, whatever you ask for in prayer, believe that you have received it, and it will be yours.'"*

Here's the key. Jesus is teaching about prayer. He's teaching people to pray, but Jesus does not want you to pray this way: "Lord, I need help. I don't know if you will even bother to respond to this prayer, but I'm praying anyway." This is not the mind of God for his people. That is not how you are supposed to pray. That is not how you approach God. There is supposed to be some sense of expectation. Why are you praying if there is no sense of expectation in your prayer?

If you are not expecting something, what are you doing but filling the air with worthless words? God wants you to be expectant. He says, *"When you pray, believe that you have received it."* You're supposed to have an anticipation that when you come to the Lord and bring before him a request or a petition, God is not just up there kicking dirt and saying, "Oh, I'm not going to listen today. I'm too busy to even pay attention to you." You're supposed to believe that God will respond to what you're petitioning.

"Ask, and you will receive...maybe" is how we live it. Jesus said, "Ask, and you will receive," but we've rewritten Matthew. "Ask, and you will receive...could be; possibly; don't know; maybe; well, who knows." That's not the way it says it. That's not the attitude, disposition, or spirit you're supposed to have when you approach God.

I come before the Lord. Sometimes, I pray, and I am so guilty of this. I just pray the prayer because you kind of know you're supposed to pray. Have you ever done that? You just know you're supposed to pray for something. Well, one time, I prayed for somebody. It was a physical situation, and I prayed for them. Now, do you think I expected them to get well? "O Lord, just fix them and heal them and do whatever you're going to do. In Jesus' name, amen." The person called me back the next day. "Guess what?"

"What?"

"I'm well."

"You're well? How could you be well?"

The person said, "Well, you prayed for me."

I said, "What does that have to do with it? How could you be well?" See, our mentality is we don't expect. We have no anticipation.

Wait, because it's going to get worse as we dive in. You've heard this story before, and you'll hear it again, about Hudson Taylor, a great missionary to China. It's a great story because it illustrates the heart of a praying man.

When the ship was blown off course and about to go into the islands where there were cannibals, the captain came in and said, "We hear you're a praying man. Will you pray that the winds will kick up so we can catch the tack and get out of here? Otherwise, we're all going to be barbecue on a stick." Hudson Taylor said, "I will only start praying if you put the sails up."

Now, you have to stop and think about that. What is this man of God saying? He's saying, "I am not even going to respond to your request, even though it's my own life unless you are in agreement for some sense of expectation. Put the sails up, pal, and then I'll pray." Under a half hour later, so let's say 20 minutes, the guy comes back in. The captain knocks on the door.

He goes, "Are you praying?" He says, "Yes." He goes, "Stop. The wind is so powerful we're having difficulty controlling the ship." You see, what's happening is a man who's seeking God is praying with expectation. "I will not pray until you put the sails on the ship up so we can demonstrate to God we believe." That's what he's saying.

Back to the text in Luke. I want to share with you our typical response. Knowing that you are just like the disciples should bring you great comfort. Verse 5: ***"Simon answered, 'Master...'"*** This did not come out poetically. I am absolutely convinced this was as whiny as whiny gets. ***"...we've worked hard all night and haven't caught anything."***

Isn't that our response to God? "I've been praying all night, God, and I ain't got squat." That's what we do. "I have been seeking, and there's nothing going on here."

Peter says, "We have spent nine hours putting nets in the water and picking up nothing but rocks and fish that were *this* big. What? Do you want me to do this more? Do you want me to be expectant after such disappointment? Do you want me to still have a heart and a mind of expectancy after being disappointed repeatedly? Do you not know, Jesus, that the proverb says, ***'Hope deferred makes the heart sick'***?"

That's us, just waiting on God. Hope deferred. "Let's go, Mister Molasses. We're waiting. Come on." It gets long, and it gets long, and it gets long, and you get discouraged. Do you not get discouraged? You do, too. You're just like me. You pray about something. You pray, you pray, and you pray. You start knocking on heaven, going, "Hello. Is anybody home?" You know, you can't figure out what's happening.

So, this is what Peter says. "Man, we've been doing this all night." But here is the key for you, for me, and for everybody who names the name of Christ in truth and sincerity. Here we come immediately into the key of what Jesus wants us to learn. Look at what Peter says. ***"Master, we've worked hard all night and haven't caught anything. <u>But because you say so, I will let down the nets.</u>"***

"Even though I am thoroughly disappointed, even though I am discouraged, even though hope deferred makes the heart sick (and my heart is not just sick; it's dead), even though I am all the way at this realm, still, Jesus, because you say to put out the net, I will put out the net again." **That's the key**. That's it.

Even though it's frustrating, to submit to the Lord's commands, to again put that net out in that water even though you haven't caught a single thing—that is the key to making the Lord move in concert with you. I want you to turn to Hebrews 10:35-36: ***"So do not throw away your confidence; it will be richly rewarded. You need to persevere so that when you have done the will of God, you will receive what he has promised."***

*Endurance*. You must endure, or you must have endurance. The King James says *patience*. Ooh, ow. That hurt. Didn't that hurt? Here, we'll read it the King James way. "You need to have patience so that when you've done the will of God, you might receive the promise." Ow. Who wants that? I'm not a doctor. I don't want patients. I mean, it's like, "Yow! Get away, get away."

But this is what the Scripture is saying. You need to have endurance. You need to have perseverance. You need to have patience. You need to have stick-to-itiveness. You need to really hang in there. You need not to quit. You need not to give up. You need not to bow down. You need not to suck water. You need to go forward. You need not to quit. You need to do all that the Lord has brought before you to do, and then when you've done it, you need to hang in there until God responds.

You think, "Well, that could be a long time." Too bad. It doesn't matter how long it is. The will of God will eventually be manifest. You have a position. You do what the Lord has put before you and don't move. You don't quit. I'm sorry, but the story, no matter how many times told, is the turtle still wins the race. He doesn't quit. He doesn't give up. He just keeps walking like *this*, piece by piece, slowly but surely, but he wins, and he finishes the race.

It's a matter of endurance and patience and prevailing with God. So many times, I've prayed and... Do you guys do this? Something comes your way, and you pray about it, and then you don't get an answer in 24 hours, so it's time to help God because God is getting old. He misplaced your file, and you need to help him because he's busy. You know, He has the stuff in Iran and Iraq. He's worried about the prophecies there. So we'll just help God along with the answer.

You're just like your forefather Abraham, who gets a promise that he's going to receive a child by promise through his wife. They wait for twelve years, and there's no kid. So, what do they do? I don't know what they thought, because they didn't know of many other lands. You know, "God is sun tanning somewhere. Why don't we help out?" So his wife Sarah says, "I'll tell you what. Here's Hagar. She's my slave. Go sleep with her. We'll get the kid. The promise of God will come to pass."

That's what we do. ***We do that all the time***. That is not exclusive to great saints. That's exclusive to *all* saints. We help God along. So what happens? They have a child. The child's name is Ishmael. Ishmael comes along. Then, after the time that God allows, here comes little Isaac, and now Ishmael is persecuting Isaac.

So, when they went to help God out by advancing his promises, they created a detriment to the actual promise of God, a problem for it. Now God has to come in and say, "Hey, get rid of *your* solution, which is Ishmael, because *my* solution is the one you're supposed to have." What we do is we create Ishmaels in our lives. Then God's promise comes along. Then we have to dump the Ishmael, and we're like, "What a bozo move *this* turned out to be."

The answer is not to help God complete His promises. He's more than adequate, more than efficient. You just need to do what He has put before you and wait until He brings it to pass. That's your job because if you help it, you will get rid of an Ishmael. You're going to be sorry. Don't do that.

Why would you do that? Isn't the lesson good enough in the Old Testament? What, you want to bear witness to it in your own life, too? Come on! That's not the heart and mind of God. Do what the Lord puts before you. Pray, don't quit, don't give up, and wait until the Lord responds.

Back to the text. Look at verses 6 and 7, because this is the result. Now, I have a terrific Bible story coming up that's one of my absolute favorites on the whole planet. Verse 6. This is when Peter had yielded to the Lord.

*"When they had done so, they caught such a large number of fish that their nets began to break. So they signaled their partners in the other boat to come and help them, and they came and filled both boats so full that they began to sink."*

So, here God is responding, and it is such a powerful response that one... It takes a lot to sink a boat. I don't know if you've been boating. To make a boat go down like *this* takes a lot. This is two boats. There are so many fish... They're probably freaking out as to how they're going to get from the water to the land. It's like, "We've got to get these fish in here. Oh, man! We're going down. Paddle fast. Hurry!"

There's such an abundant response from the Lord. So many of us think God is this stingy God. He's cutting you just enough. It's like God has this big piece of salami or something, and you want a piece of salami, and God gives you this thin little line off the slice. "Here you go. There you go. Eat on that, baby. That'll do you. There you go. Hey, call when you need more."

Ephesians 3:20 says, ***"Now unto him that is able to do exceedingly abundantly above all that we ask or think, according to the riches that are in Christ Jesus, to Him be glory throughout all ages, world without end."***

This passage in Ephesians 3:20 says it is ***"now unto Him praise who is able to do exceedingly, abundantly above all that we ask or think."*** God will do all that you petition Him for, even more than you have asked him.

He will be even more gracious than you've ever sought Him for because He's a compassionate, giving, loving, merciful God. He's not the stingy image that man has created Him to be, which some of us have gotten from our earthly fathers, some from our earthly mothers, and some from other authority figures, and we figure God is either the sheriff, the tightwad, the meany, the *this*, the *that*. None of those images of God are right.

God is generous and full of love, giving where people have not given to him, even to those who hate him. That's the kind of God you are serving, and he's pouring it out on his people more than they even know. Acts, chapter 12: I daresay the crowning glory and, without a doubt, the church's witness. I want you to follow this, because this is very powerful.

*"It was about this time that King Herod arrested some who belonged to the church, intending to persecute them. He had James, the brother of John, put to death with the sword. When he saw that this pleased the Jews, he proceeded to seize Peter also. This happened during the Feast of Unleavened Bread. After arresting him, he put him in prison, handing him over to be guarded by four squads of four soldiers each. Herod intended to bring him out for public trial after the Passover. So Peter was kept in prison, but the church was earnestly praying to God for him."*

The church was praying. What a novel idea. They take James, a key leader in the church. They eighty-six him. He's gone. Herod thinks, "Cool! They like me for it." So they grab Peter. "Eighty-six *this* guy, and they'll like me even more." Peter is in jail. The church is praying. Verse 6: *"The night before Herod was to bring him to trial, Peter was sleeping between two soldiers, bound with two chains..."* What was Peter doing sleeping the night before they were going to chop his head off? He had a good faith in God.

*"...and sentries stood guard at the entrance. Suddenly an angel of the Lord appeared and a light shone in the cell. He struck Peter on the side and woke him up. 'Quick, get up!' he said, and the chains fell off Peter's wrists. Then the angel said to him, 'Put on your clothes and sandals.' And Peter did so. 'Wrap your cloak around you and follow me,' the angel told him.*

*Peter followed him out of the prison, but he had no idea that what the angel was doing was really happening; he thought he was seeing a vision. They passed the first and second guards and came to the iron gate leading to the city. It opened for them by itself..."* I always love that line. You know, they come to the gate, and it opens. It's classic. It's like total science fiction right there.

*"It opened for them by itself, and they went through it. When they had walked the length of one street, suddenly, the angel left him. Then Peter came to himself and said, 'Now I know without a doubt that the Lord sent his angel and rescued me from Herod's clutches and from everything the Jewish people were anticipating.'*

*When this had dawned on him, he went to the house of Mary the mother of John, also called Mark, where many people had gathered and were praying. Peter knocked at the outer entrance, and a servant girl named Rhoda came to answer the door. When she recognized Peter's voice, she was so overjoyed she ran back without opening it and exclaimed, 'Peter is at the door!' 'You're out of your mind,' they told her."*

They're praying for Peter to be released. So, Peter gets released. What's their response? "You're nuts. What do you mean he's released?" I can't believe nobody in the group said, "Well, weren't we praying for that?" I can't believe it never came up. They're praying for Peter to get released. Then he gets released, and they're going, "No way. No way. Not a reality." Do you see the mental checkout that just took place there?

They are not comprehending that God is answering their prayers. Why? Because they're not anticipating or expecting God to say, "Yes." Then it happens and blows their socks off. Of course, we've mentioned how funny this is for Peter, who has just escaped prison. He's knocking on the door, and Rhoda goes to the door. "It's me. It's Peter." She turns around and runs back, and Peter is still outside...a prisoner, knocking. "Hello. Hello. Open the door. Open the door. Open the door. Open the door really fast. I think I hear horses. Come on."

We'll just take a few seconds because it's too much fun, and I cannot pass it up. Right after they tell her, "You're out of your mind..." Look at verse 15. *"'You're out of your mind,' they told her. When she kept insisting that it was so..."* See that word *insisting*? She is arguing with them whether Peter is at the door. Are you following that? Verse 16: *"But Peter kept on knocking..."* They're in one room, fighting, and he's out there knocking. She's insisting, and they're going, "It's his angel. You're nuts."

"No, it's Peter."

"No."

"Yes, it is."

"No, it isn't."

"Yes, it is."

"No, it isn't."

And Peter is still out there. I can just see heaven. What a roar. I mean, the angels are probably going, "Oy vey! That's classic." The problem with this situation is they did not expect God to say, "Yes," so they couldn't believe it. That is not the mind God wants his people to have. He wants his people to have an attitude and a mind of expectation. Let's close with these next couple of verses. Look at verse 8, because I think this is a classic, humble response when you see God moving in your life at a heavy level.

Verse 8: *"When Simon Peter saw this, he fell at Jesus' knees and said, 'Go away from me, Lord; I am a sinful man!'"* I think when you are in a place where you're praying, and God is answering, there is that overwhelming sense of feeling unworthy and feeling like, when God is at work, "Wow! Who am I that he's even answering?" There's that true human sense that you're not worthy to have God step in and change the universe on your behalf, but He does it anyway.

Verses 10 and 11 are the closing and the dual commitment. *"Then Jesus said to Simon, 'Don't be afraid; from now on you will catch men.'"* This is the divine commitment. See? Simon said, *"Jesus, go away from me because I am not worthy of you,"* but Jesus replied, *"Don't be afraid."* That "Don't be afraid" directly references Simon's request for Jesus to depart.

Jesus' response to Simon is, "Don't be afraid. I'm not leaving you. I am never leaving you. Don't be afraid. Even though you feel unworthy, even though you walk and don't feel like you're meeting the standard, do not be afraid, because I am never departing from you. Never!"

Then that next line is one of the all-time classics. *"...from now on you will catch men."* Jesus didn't mean, "You will catch men apart from me." He meant, "We will work in concert together. We will work together, spreading this gospel." The promise, or the divine commitment, is "Never be afraid; I'm not going to leave you," and "We're going to work together forever." It's a powerful, beautiful portrayal of the commitment.

Verse 11 is our proper response to that: *"So they pulled their boats up on shore, left everything and followed him."* A proper response to the commitment, passion, compassion, generosity, and grace God has for you as an individual is to make the pursuit of Jesus your highest priority in life. Matthew 6:33 says, *"Seek first the kingdom of God, and everything else will be added unto you."*

When you make the pursuit of Jesus your number-one priority, God makes the rest of your life *his* priority. That's the way to set it upright. I've got news for you. He can do a lot better job than you can. If you don't think so, just look at yourself in the mirror, and then you'll know I'm right. God is faithful. He'll take care of everything else if you seek and pursue Him first.

Isn't that hot? It's a little story that the Lord is trying to teach us to have an expectant heart. When the Lord does respond, we should have a humble response, but He wants us to know He will never leave us, He will never forsake us, and He will never dump us. It will never happen. Our response should be taking our boats, pulling them up on shore, leaving everything, and saying, "I am going to follow Jesus." Let's pray.

# Chapter 10
# THE GTAC CAMPAIGN

I trust the Lord that He will go beyond me to you in this chapter. I believe it is imperative for us as the people of God to move from a 6 to a 9. By that, I mean that our place, mindsets, and hearts are moved up the ladder.

Some of you know I do a run from time to time. I go into the garage and either close the garage or tune out the universe and run. It's a great prayer time for me. And in case you're wondering, the title of this chapter is *The GTAC Campaign*. It doesn't stand for "God's Thermal Air Conditioning." You might think it might, but it doesn't. I just want to point that out to you ...right off the bat.

Anyway, the Lord is with me, and I'm running and praying. When I run, I run for an hour. That's what I do. Some runs are better than others. I'm sitting there and going over another teaching in my mind. As I pray to the Lord and huffing along, I think about the message. I'm communing with God, saying, "What about *this*?"

What I do is I think about what I'm going to communicate, and I bring it to the Lord. I literally meditate on it with Him in prayer. He's right beside me, sitting in a chair, laughing at me because I'm running. I talk to Him, like, "What about *this*? What about *that*?" So,

I'm running and running, and all of a sudden, while I'm running... If I could describe it, I would describe it as a wave.

A wave comes in and hits me, almost like an invisible ocean. Fears out of left field start attacking me. I'm running, and I'm thinking, "I know just a second ago I was talking to You about this other teaching. What is this whole barrage of thoughts?" All of a sudden, as I'm running, these thoughts of fear, darkness, and doubt start slamming against me one after the other.

Now, I'm not a genius, but I know five seconds ago I was running, and I could be in pain from running, but it does not cause *this*. All of a sudden, in my mind, conclusions that are down the road, the scenarios I'm seeing down the road are turning dark, almost like a foreboding. You know how you think, "What's around the corner?" but you have that negative connotation or "Well, I'm just waiting for the other shoe to drop" kind of mentality, that whole disposition? "Now that *this* has happened, *this* must happen."

What happens a lot for us is the Lord will bring us into a hard place, and then we struggle through and get out, and then we start getting into a better place. As soon as you get into that better place, that little part of you thinks, "I'm not worthy of this. I'm not worth this. I don't deserve this." So then you think, "Therefore, something else must happen to come and compensate to bring the whole thing into balance. It must be bad because right now, I'm feeling good." Has anybody ever gone through that experience? I know you have.

These thoughts were continuous, like a bombardment. It was like a wave. *Boom. Boom. Boom.* First it was like fears, then general doubting, and then it was kind of like darkness. Then, the conclusions to things that are up and coming were horrible. I'm sitting there thinking, "What is going on?" Then that foreboding.

So, I want you to look with me at the Gospel of John, chapter 10, verse 10, and we'll talk about this particular experience and what to do. John 10:10: ***"The thief comes only to steal and kill and destroy; I have come that they may have life, and have it to the full."*** What we know for sure is the thief comes to kill, to steal, to destroy, to bring destruction, to bring doubt, to bring fears, and it's fears that are, I would almost say, plausible but irrational.

You think down a scenario two, three, or four years down the road, and suddenly, you're anticipating what will happen in four years. You don't even know what will happen in four minutes, but you find yourself fighting for what's happening four years from now. There might not be a four years from now. That's the great irony of the whole system. There might not be a four hours from now. We don't know.

The best way to describe it to you... The most brutally honest way I can say it to you is it starts with the fears, and then the fears step into the realm of doubts. Doubts have now eliminated faith, and when your fears start taking over, and your doubt starts sucking down the faith, then the darkness comes right behind it.

I realized, "I'm in a war right now." While I was running, as I was thinking about the other teachings and what they are, I thought, "This is out of left field. This shouldn't exist because I was in a different place." That's when it dawned on me, while I was running, that Satan was attacking my expectations. I'd never labeled it that way before, but that's exactly what it was.

He was attacking the faith I was using for the future, for not a fearful future...a great future, a wonderful future in God, hope, happiness, and anticipation. He was coming in and trying to disrupt and pervert. He was attacking my expectations. So, you think, "What's the answer?" Well, the answer to that and every question you ever have is in 1 Corinthians, chapter 15. This won't be a perfectly spoken message, but you're done if you get what God gave me. You'll be moving on, and that'll be the key.

So, the first thing is I'm in a warfare, and I recognize I'm in a warfare. Even though I'm in warfare, will David's power prevail? No. "Oh, you really know your Bible, Dave." I don't know squat. The Devil knows the Bible a thousand times better than I do. He has been around a lot longer, and he knows everything it has to say. He can quote any verse anywhere, anytime. I can't. He can quote the whole thing in a sitting. I can't. He knows it. He's not unaware of it.

"So, is it your powerful prayer life?" Don't make me and God laugh. What powerful prayer life? "Is it any of those things?" It has nothing to do with me. The fact that I ever have a victory is sheerly the grace of God. But here is the answer. First Corinthians 15:57. If you don't have this marked, you should. ***"But thanks be to God! He gives us the victory through our Lord Jesus Christ."***

It's in connotation and context to sin, it's in connotation and context to death, but it is applicable to every situation in your life. You say, "How do you know that's true?" Romans 8:37 says, "In all these things we are more than conquerors," and 2 Corinthians 2:14 says, "Thanks be unto God, who always leads us in triumphal procession." So we know it's replete throughout Scripture. Oh, yeah, and then Paul said, "I can do all things through Christ." I mean, there's plenty to back it up, but the point is victory is in Jesus.

So, I'm sitting there, running, and going, "This doesn't seem right." I'm running, like, "I know there's victory in Jesus. I know there's victory in Jesus." I was like, "I come against that. I don't receive that. I don't receive the fear. I'm not going to hang on to this fear. I'm not going to give strength to this fear. I'm not going to empower these doubts. I won't let this darkness sweep on the top of my head. I'm not going to do it. I'm not going to give up, Lord. I'm not going to change my mindset."

Remember the story with Elijah? Elijah goes to hear the voice of God. He goes to the mountain, and there's a powerful earthquake, but the Lord doesn't speak. There are flames, and the Lord doesn't speak. There are noises and this and that. The Lord doesn't speak. But then this quiet, gentle whisper comes, and Elijah knows, "Now God is going to speak." He goes out to hear the Lord.

So, I'm running, and I quiet my mind. I rebuke every fearful and doubtful thought. I do not take personal ownership. I do not accept it. I refuse to accept it. I turn my eyes to the Lord and say, "Look. You're my victory, You're my answer, You're my solution, and I am focused on you. I'm not going anywhere else. I'm going to believe You. I'm not going to accept this other garbage." That's exactly what I said.

Then the Lord whispered. Do you know what the Lord said to me? Yes, I said it was God who did that. The Lord said, "Great things are coming." I thought, "Hot dog!" I just went through this experience of battle and warfare, and I just said, "No, I'm not going to let this go; I'm not going to drop this," the Lord speaks to me and says, "Great things are coming."

When the enemy is sitting there, whispering in my ear, "It's going to turn to garbage. It's going to blow up in your face. It's *this*, and it's *that*..." "No! No! I'm not going to accept that." Finally, when the voices are quiet, and I'm no longer talking louder than everybody else, and the Devil is no longer speaking, and the truth has been spoken, in a whisper, God tells me, "Great things are coming."

I'm running, and I'm thinking, "Woo dog! That's some hot stuff right there. I can live off of that the rest of my life." So, now you understand why it's the *GTAC Campaign*. Great Things Are Coming...GTAC. That's what it stands for. I want to tell you right now, right this second... I've been doing this for years. I have felt invigorated and charged up.

Whenever something negative pops through this large empty space, I immediately say, "Great things are coming. Great things are coming." The Devil is like... "Nope. Great things are coming. God said great things are coming. Nope. I'm not even going to hear it. I don't even want to hear it. Nope. I don't care. Great things are coming."

You think, "Well, can you do that forever?" I don't know. I'm going to try. I don't know. I think you should try it too. I think you should walk out of this building today, and I think every time it happens, you should just say, "Great things are coming." Then I realized how powerful this is. It's a little more powerful than even I thought at first. Then I thought, "How do I teach this?"

I'm going to teach you really quickly. We'll buzz through a few things because you want to know it's based on Scripture. You sure do. Go to Mark 11:20. We're going to go through about four Scriptures, and they're not even going to be complex. We will review them, look at them, and recognize them.

Here is the message for this book. This is the message you should highlight. If you never highlight, you should highlight this: *great things are coming*. I mean, we're in a company right now that... Just to give you an idea, we went down and had a successful business trip for our software process.

Mark 11:20. Not a lot of complexity. I just want you to understand this one thing. I want you to understand the power of expectation and why this is important for you. Mark, chapter 11, starting in verse 20, out of the NIV, says this:

***"In the morning, as they went along, they saw the fig tree withered from the roots. Peter remembered and said to Jesus,***

*'Rabbi, look! The fig tree you cursed has withered!' 'Have faith in God,' Jesus answered. 'I tell you the truth, if anyone says to this mountain, "Go, throw yourself into the sea," and does not doubt in his heart but believes that what he says will happen, it will be done for him. Therefore I tell you, whatever you ask for in prayer, believe that you have received it, and it will be yours.'"*

The power of expectation. Jesus is teaching his disciples, "Hey, when you pray and ask for something, you must believe that that is in Reception City for your life." Now, that doesn't mean you don't keep praying, because Jesus taught us the principles of persistent prayer, but what it means is you persist because you believe until you receive, and then you spend that same amount of energy being thankful instead of just going on to your next project.

You should have an expectancy. I should have an expectancy. We should be an expectant people. Why? Oh, we're going to talk about why. I could do a thousand Scriptures. How many of you remember me talking about Hudson Taylor, the Hudson Taylor story, missionary to China? We call it the *Hudson Taylor tale* because we don't know exactly how it happened, and the story has been told a hundred times, and it kind of varies.

In a nutshell, he's in a boat. He was going to China. He was going to be a missionary to China, on his way. They had no wind, and the ship was drifting toward an island. The only problem was, apparently, the island was an island full of what they anticipated or thought maybe cannibals, so probably not the kind of island you want to land on.

So, they were floating that way, and the captain came to Hudson Taylor and said, "I understand that you're a praying man, a man of God who believes God does miracles." He said, "I am." The captain said, "I want you to pray that the Lord will bring us wind." Hudson

Taylor said, "No. Not until you put the sails up. Then I'll pray for the wind because if you put the sails up, you'll believe that wind is coming."

The idea of the story is that you put the sails up first, and then you pray for the wind. It's expecting the answer. You think, "Well, how scriptural is that really?" I don't know. Let's look at Matthew, chapter 8, and see. I could do this 30 times, but let's just do some of the better ones, because I like them. Matthew, chapter 8. We're going to start with verse 5. Has anybody ever heard of the centurion? Let's talk about the centurion. He's in several of the Gospels. Matthew 8:5:

*"When Jesus had entered Capernaum, a centurion came to him, asking for help. 'Lord,' he said, 'my servant lies at home paralyzed and in terrible suffering.' Jesus said to him, 'I will go and heal him.' The centurion replied, 'Lord, I do not deserve to have you come under my roof. But just say the word, and my servant will be healed. For I myself am a man under authority, with soldiers under me. I tell this one, "Go," and he goes; and that one, "Come," and he comes. I say to my servant, "Do this," and he does it.'*

*When Jesus heard this, he was astonished and said to those following him, 'I tell you the truth, I have not found anyone in Israel with such great faith. I say to you that many will come from the east and the west, and will take their places at the feast with Abraham, Isaac and Jacob in the kingdom of heaven. But the subjects of the kingdom will be thrown outside, into the darkness, where there will be weeping and gnashing of teeth.' Then Jesus said to the centurion, 'Go! It will be done just as you believed it would.' And his servant was healed at that very hour."*

Hello! I mean, look. "Go. It's going to happen just the way you believed." And it did. Do you get that? That's the expectancy. "Go. It will happen just how you believed it would happen." "You got it, man. I'm with you, God. Let's go. You and me a partnership, you and me a majority. It's all that matters."

"Ah, but the world and the church say *this*." Well, don't listen to the world; if the church says something contrary to Jesus, don't listen to the church. Listen to Jesus. "Go. It'll be done just as you believed." "Really?" Yeah. That's the whole point. That's why great things are coming. You say, "I don't believe that." Well, then, great things aren't coming for you. They're coming for me. I believe it 100 percent. Great things are coming. You think, "I've got to get that faith." Well, get in the Book and start reading all of the stories where it happens.

I want to talk about the key principle of understanding this. It's in Matthew, chapter 9. You don't have to go very far. Matthew 9:27. The key principle: the blind men. ***"As Jesus went on from there, two blind men followed him, calling out, 'Have mercy on us, Son of David!' When he had gone indoors, the blind men came to him, and he asked them, 'Do you believe that I am able to do this?'"***

I want you to know right now that is the question God asks you every time you pray. "Do you believe I'm able to do this?" Why? Because if you don't believe, don't bother. You either pray with faith, believing, or don't pray. Don't pray out of obligation. You're not impressing God. Pray because you believe. Pray because you trust your partnership with God. Pray because you love him.

***"'Yes, Lord,' they replied."*** Verse 29 and the key principle: ***"Then he touched their eyes and said, 'According to your faith will it be done to you...'"*** You think I was kidding just a second ago when I said, "Great things are coming, and if you don't believe it, then they're not coming for you." No. That's exactly true. If you don't believe it, it isn't happening for you.

If your faith says, "No," the answer is "No." God will work with you and me only to the level of our faith because faith is the vehicle He has chosen to interact with us. If we don't believe, just like Jesus couldn't do many miracles there because of their unbelief, we're shutting God down. Or we could take the opposite tack and say, "No, I believe. Not only do I believe; I believe He can open up the eyes of the blind." And they were opened.

Jesus laid out the principle. "According to your faith, so be it. According to your faith, be it done unto you." Why? Well, because God wants you to believe He can, will, and does. He doesn't want you to be like, "O Lord, please heal this person." Don't even bother. "God, I'm in a terrible financial situation, and I know you love me and are going to take care of me." Don't even.

From a financial point of view, I will tell you a statistic nobody has ever shared on the radio or in this church. When it talks about all of the different miracles in the gospel, not including the resurrection... When it talks about the different miracles in the Bible, did you know that only one creative miracle is in all four gospels as a self-separated miracle? It's the miracle of the feeding of the 5,000.

I find it ironic that the only miracle in Matthew, Mark, Luke, and John consistently is when Jesus takes little, gives thanks, gives it away, and multiplies. Hello! Principle. Thought process. Like, "Wow! Why did He have to say that so many times?" Because He wants us to get it, not miss it.

Remember Oral Roberts? Remember his campaign? "Expect a miracle." People laughed, and they ridiculed, and they made fun of him. He had big ears. And He did, so you can't do anything about that. He was an okay teacher but did one thing better than others. He moved people's level of expectation in God higher, because He just came up with three words: "Expect a miracle." Like, wow! That seems so simple. Yeah, but it's good.

You think, "Well, I don't like Oral Roberts, and I don't like his teachings." Do you think saying, "Expect a miracle" is bad? Start reading your Bible, because you don't know anything. Jesus wants us to expect a miracle. He just came up with the phrase faster and kind of coined it and then marketed it, which was... You know, that's what he did. In the same token, I am telling you... That campaign is a brilliant campaign. That campaign affects so many people.

Guess what? Great things are coming. That's the next campaign. Great things are coming. What's around the corner? I don't know, but it's great. I don't care. I mean, I don't know. It's just great. Picking out the land now. Start surveying. Start believing. Start trusting. Start living your life that way instead of thinking about it. You think, "Well, Dave, that seems so..." You know I'm very anti "name it and claim it" but a very "believe the Word of God and do it" kind of person.

Mark, chapter 10. Here's what I'm going to tell you. I was reading this a couple of weeks back and was excited about it. I don't know what it was. It just struck me as weird. Here's what I'm going to say to you. What we need to do, as individuals and as a body, is keep our expectations high.

I will tell you why...because of Mark 10:27. This is in reference to the rich young man. Jesus is responding. He says, "It's hard for rich people to get saved," they're all like, "Oh, who can get saved?" Blah, blah, blah. They're all freaking out because of Jesus' teaching. Verse 27: ***"Jesus looked at them and said, 'With man this is impossible, but not with God; all things are possible with God.'"***

Do you want to know why we should keep our level of expectation high? Because all things are possible with God. You think, "Well, that's possibility teaching." No, that's actually Mark 10:27. Jesus said that in three other places in the Gospels. I didn't write the book, but the Book is the Book.

We should keep our level of expectation high because all things are possible with God. We would be different people if we just got those six words and imprinted them in our brains. "All things are possible with God. I'm going through this. All things are possible with God. This is a tough one. All things are possible with God." You're like, "Okay." So, great things are coming.

Let me close with this. I love this. These are two great portions that you have to appreciate. John 1:16. This goes to the very heart and nature of who God is, which you must appreciate. Listen to this. Listen to how beautiful this is. Look at the heart of God. ***"From the fullness of his grace, we have all received one blessing after another."*** Now, in context, it has to do with salvation, but you have to keep in mind that salvation has a lot to do with redemption, and redemption has a lot to do with everything.

We receive one blessing after another because of the fullness of God's grace in our lives. You don't receive all these blessings because you're worthy. You're not. You receive them because of the fullness of his grace because he's generous. It's like the parable with the guy who throws the wedding, and then people are too busy to come to the party. "All right. Go out to the highways." And they're too busy. Finally, they fill out...

It's like somebody who wants to throw a party and give people a blessing. Back then, they used to give presents at weddings, which they do in Japan now. When they have a wedding, they actually give *you* presents. Somebody wants to throw a party for people, and nobody wants to come. God is going, "What's wrong with you people? I'm here to give to you. What are you doing?"

Let's close with Romans, chapter 8. You can't do better than this. I don't think you can do better than this. Again, the general context is salvation and redemption, but the application is obvious. *The GTAC Campaign*. Great things...not even good things...great things are coming. I mean, how do you not love that? Right? I will live that until I'm done, and then I will see even more great things.

Romans 8:32: ***"He who did not spare his own Son, but gave him up for us all—how will he not also, along with him, graciously give us all things?"*** Do you get the generosity, graciousness, and giving disposition that's from the heart of God when you read that? You bet. Does that apply to your life? I don't know. Is your life important to God? If it is, then it applies.

You think, "Well, I'm not good enough." You're right. You're not, but because Jesus died for you and the Holy Spirit lives in you, you qualify under another clause. It's called the *"God chose you" clause*. So, you're chosen beyond your ability to earn it, and now your big mission in life is to receive it. That's your big mission: receive it. Let's pray.

# Chapter 11
# About Dr. David Spoon

D r. David Spoon was born and raised in a Jewish home in Detroit, Michigan. He attended a private Hebrew school called Hillel Hebrew Academy. David was bar mitzvahed at the age of thirteen. Not long after, he was involved in drug abuse and trafficking. After hearing the Gospel for the first time at age seventeen, David accepted Jesus Christ as his Lord and Savior. A few months later, David had a dramatic experience with God. Immediately set free from years of excessive drug use, he committed himself to ministry and to furthering the Kingdom of God.

He graduated from Life Pacific College Summa-cum-Laude in their Ministry and Leadership program. He graduated with honors from Regent University with a master's degree in theological studies and completed his Doctor of Ministry program in Strategic Christian Ministry at Liberty University.

David is married to his best friend, Noelle. He has three children and seven grandchildren, plus a dog named Bert. On March 18th, 2019, he started "The David Spoon Experience" in Texas.

He is the President of He Must Increase Ministry, a 501c3 ministry and hosts the live daily radio show "The David Spoon Experience" through DJR Broadcasting on the 770 A.M. radio dial, throughout different states, on various apps, and on the Internet. David is a Jewish-Christian, Bapti-Costal, Cal-Minian, Manifold Millennialist. Just ask him.

# Chapter 12
# Other Books by Dr. David Spoon

**B**ROKEN...FOR HIS GLORY!

*Not all Churches are bad, but not all Churches are Good!*

This book is for anyone engaged in a church as a servant, leader, member, or attendee who feels misplaced, lost, and confused and wonders about God's plan. Has a church hurt you?

Award-winning author, radio host, and former pastor David Spoon presents his book "BROKEN FOR HIS GLORY" to explore this question.

Dr. Spoon uses his own challenging church experiences as a catalyst to educate others. He transforms his youthful struggles with drug addiction, subsequent conversion to Christianity, and the pain inflicted by a church into a personal Journey aimed at assisting readers in resolving and recuperating from their spiritual conflicts.

By linking the stages of Jesus' sufferings to Christians who have endured church-related pain, Dr. Spoon demonstrates that being hurt by a church isn't a catastrophe. On the contrary, it can ultimately be beneficial.

## Other Books by Dr. David Spoon (2)

### <u>THE JEWISH CHRISTIAN!</u>

***God is knocking on the door of your heart!***

This book provides a fresh perspective through the eyes of a Jewish Christian. For too many people, Christianity falls short of being a living relationship with the living God. In this reading, you may not find all the answers to all your problems, but you will be encouraged and challenged to search deeper.

If you have never had an encounter with God, you are in for a treat. God is real, and you are not accidentally holding this book in your hands.

Each chapter is a practical guide to drawing closer to the King of the universe. Several angles are examined, but all roads point upward in the end.

What we hope you won't discover is some form of religiosity. Instead, we pray that you discover His love for you. And how deep your relationship with Him can go.